Shelvie Summerlin, Litt.D.

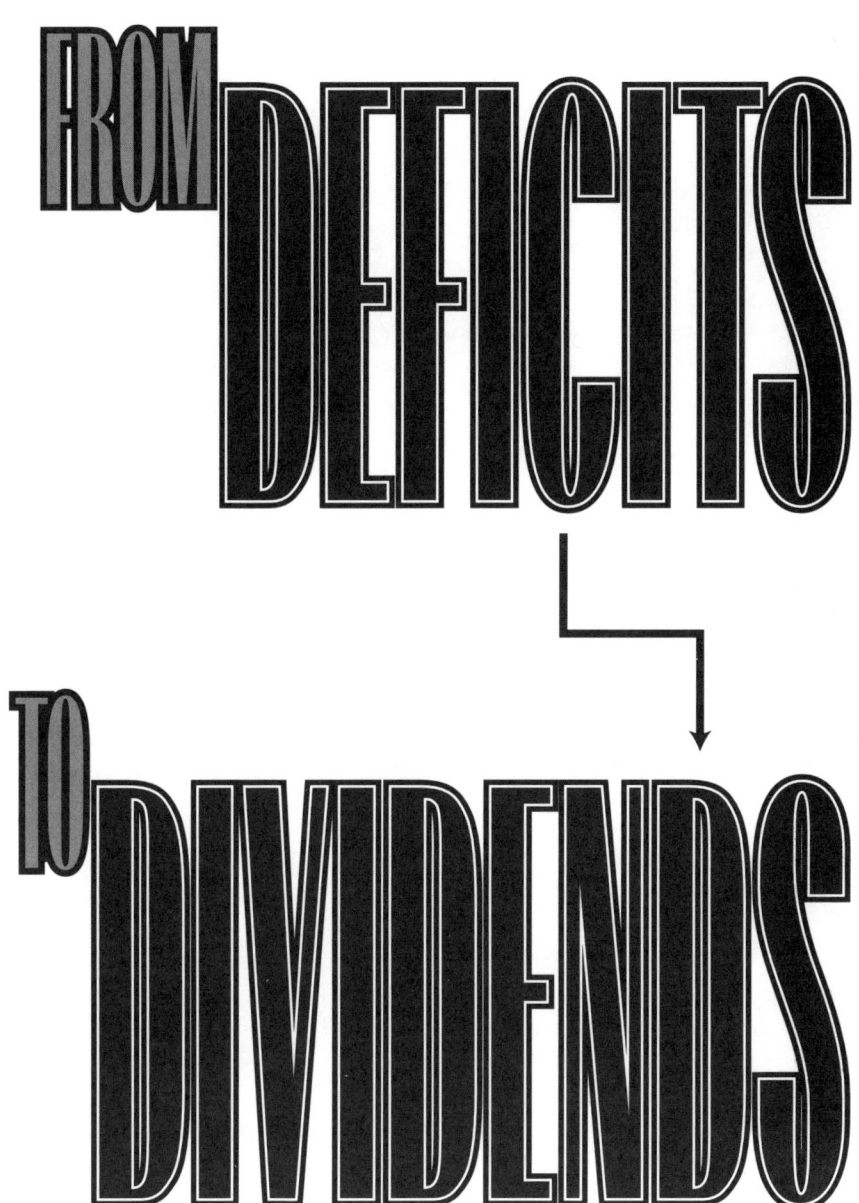

FROM DEFICITS

TO DIVIDENDS

ISBN #0-9658997-0-5

Printed by
LifeSprings Resources
P.O. Box 9
2425 W. Main St.
Franklin Springs, GA 30639

Printed in the United States of America

Dedication

This book is dedicated to the memory of a very dear friend and fellow member of the board of directors of Provident Investment Corporation, Kenneth E. Crawford. The unselfish gift of his time and resources made him a model board member.

Kenneth E. Crawford

Ken and I forged an enduring friendship under very difficult circumstances when the future of Provident appeared hopeless. But he never gave up. He was the biblical Barnabas who stood by my side when I needed a true-blue friend. We shared an unshakable trust in each other that was bonded by the cement of amity.

Many times when the company was suffering financially, he invested considerable amounts of funds with no guarantee that these funds would ever be repaid. Many of the thriving churches whose names are in the company's loans portfolio today would not be there without the help from a great Christian gentleman – Kenneth E. Crawford.

His untimely homegoing at the age of 58 vacated a chair on the directorship that has been very difficult to fill. His warm, quiet manner and personal charm are missed immensely, but I feel sure heaven is a better place since he has made the transition.

I shall ever be grateful to his charming wife, Nancy and daughters, Cathy and Gayla for their unfailing friendship and continued loyal support. They are living proof that no matter how difficult the circumstances are and how dark the night, you can "Live Again" if your faith has the proper anchor.

Shelvie and Myrtle Summerlin

Nancy and Gayla, wife and daughter of Kenneth E. Crawford.

Acknowledgements

A book should be a reservoir of thoughts and knowledge compiled in a manner that the reader may dip with his bucket and share with the author the messages contained therein. Only those who open its cover and read shall share the otherwise silent message. *From Deficits to Dividends* contains a great story about a Christian financial organization that was conceived with the idea of being a servant to churches of the Lord Jesus Christ in whatever form it exists.

There have been some rough and stormy seas that could have overwhelmed the organization and buried it within the rough sands of the sea where the tide also ebbs and flows. However, the divine mandate dictated otherwise. The servant vessel has survived to fulfill its vital ministry of providing a helping hand to the church through various methods of financing.

This reservoir would never have reached its current capacity without the contributions from the Board of Directors and others who have helped in a variety of ways by being a supply tributary. Each has unselfishly flowed into this source and has helped to bring a somewhat adequate supply. The following printed list of these spiritual tributaries is grossly incomplete, but until the true and complete report of all mankind is given by divine perogative, those inadvertently omitted will remain anonymous.

Dr. G. Herfin Taylor, a member of the board of directors who at the age of 86 continues as a firm anchor and a very dear friend. He has provided wisdom and strength in the midst of the storms that have sustained Provident until the repairs were made and the vessel could move to calmer waters.

Jonathan Ostrom who has been a loyal and supportive assistant and has possibly gone to the bank with me more times than he should. But a common cause has buoyed us during flooding waters. Thank you, mate!

To my brother, Ralph Summerlin, who has been a dear friend since childhood, who has believed in me and extended trust and faith, many times possibly when his conscience said otherwise.

To Frank Page, a loyal corporate secretary, who has set his seal and signature to countless thunderous business meeting reports when the only hope was another day. For his stately attorney appearance when the company could not afford one.

To the late Kenneth E. Crawford whose gentle smile and kind mannerism provided a ray of sunshine through many dark and fearful clouds. To his wife Nancy who wrote many checks when she surely must have quietly disagreed.

To Dewey T. Bryson, a former board member and corporate secretary whose unshakable Christian testimony met every challenge. For his deep and profound knowledge in real estate and real estate appraisals which kept us with a sound sense of values.

To Bobby Tatum, a stable board member who possesses a great sense of humor that has kept us with a smile when tears would have been much easier. For the supply of wisdom and love that was part of the great package we received when he came aboard.

To Dr. Henry Wright II, a valued advisor who pastors one of the leading churches in the Valdosta-Lowndes County area. For evidencing leadership qualities in 1992 that captured the coveted honor as "Lowndes County Man of the Year."

To Debbie Sanders, my personal secretary and youngest daughter, whose patience has rivaled the Patriarch Job. For possessing the unusual ability of being able to decipher and read her father's handwriting that no other human being would attempt. For countless hours of uncompensated time just for the sake of helping keep a vessel afloat that otherwise would have sunk.

To Betty Reese, a member of the board of directors and a lady with great intellect who must surely possess the biblical gift of "helps." Only heaven knows where she might have gone on the ladder of success if she had not spent so much of her time helping others. However, those to whom she has extended assistance would not have gone nearly so far!

To my precious wife Myrtle, who after almost 48 years of marriage, continues to lend unqualified support to a husband who has never learned to say no when there is work to be done or values to be supported or defended. For sharing a husband with six church congregations for more than 40 years and a time of half that duration leading a struggling financial organization when it would have been much easier to walk away.

Finally to "Ole Reb Dog," my faithful Labrador retriever, who saw more of me during the time of writing this treatise than any other period of his life. For being my loyal walking partner daily as three miles registered on the pedometer through the quiet woods and paths at Myrshel Lodge and farm.

Foreward

The idea of a need for a book to be written about the history of Provident Investment Corporation apparently was birthed in my deep personal friend, Reverend Shelvie Summerlin, and yours truly at about the same time. Why the wonderful Holy Spirit chose to deal with both of us at a very precise time is one of those things the literary world would call "enigmatic." Those of us who are akin to the work of the Holy Spirit know that He is much too wise to engage in fanciful conundrum.

I had no interest in writing the account that has been so wonderfully woven through the leadership of the Holy Spirit, but I possessed a deep conviction that the story should be told and preserved for the now generation and those to come, should Jesus tarry. One day, Brother Summerlin and his wife stopped by our home for a brief visit, and I shared my conviction with him about the need for a history of the organization we were leading. He listened intently as I shared my deep feelings about the matter. I was set somewhat aback when he informed me that he had shared the same conviction for some time and was in the process of writing a treatise that would preserve the story. Immediately, we both knew that the Lord's Hand was in the matter, and I began to encourage him to continue his efforts in a matter we both considered very important.

Only those who have undertaken a task so great as to write a book know the amount of time required. Brother Summerlin was already heavily loaded with the responsibilities as Chief Executive Officer of our organization that has grown under his leadership from the brink of bankruptcy to a strong seven-figure financial company. I was not sure where he would find the time for the work, but I was confident that the Lord would help him find the time element necessary for recording the story!

After almost three years of grueling writing, changing, rewriting and other matters basic to those who attempt to record the message through the pen, he has finished the work. He asked me to read each chapter as he drafted them and to offer any comments I felt would enhance the book's appeal and readability. I must confess that the changes I have recommended have been minor. The story is told in his own unique manner but in a form I think that will appeal to those who shall read about one of the great modern-day miracles – FROM DEFICITS TO DIVIDENDS!

In chapter four, he alludes to a very stormy meeting at the Georgia Securities Investigation Department, where the seven members of the Board of Directors were summoned to witness a heartbreaking revelation. We were to learn that the company we were serving was on the verge of financial calamity, and an extensive investigation was in process. It was at this frightening meeting that I nominated board member Shelvie Summerlin to take the reigns of leadership of a very troubled financial organization. He received unanimous endorsement and began on that very blusterous day to provide sound leadership for a deeply troubled company.

Those of us who have been through the fiery waters have been eyewitnesses to one of the greatest miracles of our lifetime. It took more than seven years to overcome the huge deficits that were accumulated by two previous leadership attempts. You will do yourself a great favor by reading this book and sharing with others the miracle story. It is a true-life story of a company conceived no doubt with divine implications, but run aground due to inexperienced and poor leadership. Enough said, why not turn the page and begin reading a story I don't think you will stop until you have read the final chapter.

Dr. G. Herfin Taylor

Contents

Chapter One
A Fragile Basket

I wish I knew the author who coined the phrase, "Necessity is the mother of invention." I would like to acknowledge appreciation for his deep words of wisdom and pay author's respect for their use in this treatise. Doubtless, necessity has mothered more inventions, solved more problems, made more difficult tasks easier than all other combined efforts of mankind to advance himself.

A lot of money is required to finance a worthwhile church project. Have you ever wrestled with the herculean task of obtaining a loan to fill so great a need? The enormous amount of time and work involved in securing the necessary data to satisfy a banking committee is astounding. It has always been an enigma for me to understand why bankers are so repulsive toward committing to make a loan, secured by choice real estate, well-constructed buildings and usually personally endorsed by sound Christian people. My research over a period of nearly 50 years well documents the fact that church loans have the best payoff record of all the loans on banking records.

I have finally concluded that the reasons for the "stand-off" attitude exhibited by most banking officials is due to an inherent nature to properly collateralize all loans. There is an old adage among bankers which says "Your chances are better in a tiger's den than to fool around with a banker's collateral." The plain truth about church loans is they are good banking loans. However,

1

there is the absence of collateral that a banker is comfortable with if he is forced into foreclosure procedures. Most church loans are made on the basis of the financial strength and integrity of those church officers and officials who sign and guarantee the loan.

Several years ago during the early months of the decade of the '70s, Reverend Claude Collins approached me about the problems the majority of pastors were encountering while attempting to obtain financing for churches they felt the Lord had called them to build and pastor. I gave him a very sympathetic ear because at that time I had already spent more than 20 years in home missions ministry. I was a seasoned veteran in the field of dealing with banking officials while I was attempting to obtain a loan for a church building I would not own and gave my uncompensated time and money to help make it possible. Pastor Collins told me that the Lord had helped him with an idea which he felt surely would work and provide the needed funds for churches for permanent financing of their mortgages.

My ears took the stance of an oscillating radar scope as I listened to the smooth plan offered by the commiserative preacher. The plan was simple and contained all the apparent necessary strategy to formulate and establish a stock-held institution to be financed through the sale of common stock. The stock shares were to be marketed at a cost low enough that the poorest person on earth would be able to participate. As the plan unfolded, anyone could readily detect that the strategem had divine implications, and if fostered properly, could develop into a mighty weapon in the Lord's arsenal.

My experience in stock-held corporation was extremely limited. I was working for a large stock-held corporation at the time and had participated in their employee stock plan. I had also taught Junior Achievement Classes for several years. These duties entailed a miniature version of establishing small companies, electing officers, and selling stock to raise capital. The students were required to select a product to manufacture and establish a manufacturing body to create the product. A sales force was created to market the product in a profitable manner. A complete set of records was required to record the history of the newly founded company. I was able to see and identify all the necessary components in the church financing structure my friend was presenting. It had the appearance of bearing divine clout and would be a godsend to all churches, especially those which were small and in many cases not able to present a bankable proposition to a lending institution. As I was listening to the smooth parlance of my concerned visitor, inwardly I was already nodding my approval!

Stock to be sold

The initial plan called for the issue and sale of 525,000 shares of pre-incorporation stock. This stock was to be sold for five cents per share and would prove to be the best bargain in the entire stock offering. These shares were quickly bought by the inner circle of officers and friends who were privy to the availability of this stock. These purchases were made with complete knowledge that the next offering would be marketed at twenty-five cents per share. As soon as the second offering was in the hands of eager salesmen, every share sold was more than tripling the value of the pre-inc stock, and each holder was enjoying a handsome increase in a matter of a few short weeks.

Let me hasten to say that this is a policy that is usually followed by companies and corporations which are chartered through the stock funding process. My quarrel stems from the fact that those who are approached to buy stock at a later offering are not informed as to the amount of stock outstanding which was sold at a lesser value, which in reality dilutes their stock appreciably. In the case of discussion, the 25-cent stock was worth less than 16 cents-per on the day it was purchased, while the pre-inc stock skyrocketed to 16 cents per share. A person who expects to buy stock in any firm would be wise to inquire as to the amount of stock that has been sold in previous offerings and obtain the price for which the entire stock was marketed.

The absence of information regarding the pre-inc stock did not diminish from the utopian sales pitch I was receiving from my friend. The waitress frequented the booth where we were sitting and kept our coffee cups filled with the freshly-brewed Maxwell House coffee for which that restaurant was famous. I could hardly wait until the sales dialogue was over so I could write my check to purchase some stock in this venture. I felt it was an answer to prayer and a solution to the loan obtaining problem for so many home missions pastors like me.

The engaging eyes of the preacher salesman never left their subject. Finally, the sales closing touch was added to the superb sales presentation, and in a smooth low-pitched tone he asked, "How much would you like to buy?"

My voice quickly responded with the number "Ten thousand!" I really intended to say ten thousand dollars' worth, but mercifully the mature salesman thought I meant ten thousand shares and hastily proceeded to write up the contract for the specified number of shares. Had the convincing promoter properly interpreted my intentions, I would have been the owner of 40,000 shares of Provident Investment Stock! I continue to thank the Lord for the misinterpretation of my anxious speech.

The message of the newly-formed "God-sent" miracle company spread over the state of Georgia and the Southeast like wild fire. Its conception by respectable men of considerable spiritual stature provided a premise of ease for the matter to be discussed at all church conventions and meetings. The intended mission for the infant financial institution was to cover most of the monetary loan needs of the participating bodies. Leading churchmen like Earnest P. Pruett, Gerald Balius, Charles Davis, Warren Crider, Elmer Green and others loaned their respect and influence. Some were gracious enough to offer personal endorsement to the promotional phase of the sale of stock for the purpose of raising the needed funds for church financing.

The well-conceived sales plan was to offer 20 million shares of Class A common stock at the price of 25 cents per share. This sales effort was to generate the attractive sum of almost $3 million. The company officials were authorized to act as salesmen, and a number of other men possessing great charisma and personal charm were employed on a commission basis to promote and sell the stock of the apparent bonanza banking institution. Their association with extremely respected ecclesiastical leadership provided an open door to all churches in order to discuss and promote a plan which was intended to be mutually beneficial to the stock purchaser and church with which they were affiliated. The message the salesmen promoted was a "guaranteed no-lose" situation.

The initial target of the sales force was the church pastor. The strategy was to convince the church leader of the validity and urgent need of the worthy fund-raising effort. The majority of the pastors, even though chiefly men of meager means, became easy subjects of the massive sales promotion. Many invested every available dollar in the apparently worthy entity which was designed to be a good steward of their investment. Many of those who did not have available funds, to make the near covenanted purchase, borrowed the desired amount from banks, other individuals, and lending institutions. Many of these saintly people were near, or approaching, retirement age. They were convincingly satisfied by the smooth parlance of master promoters that the company in which they were placing their life savings would return these funds, plus a handsome dividend. The tragedy in many cases was the faithful promises made by the sales blitz team that the company could and would return their money in the event of an emergency or personal need. These promises were not even remotely possible even at the time they were made. Shares of stock carry an equal value in any stock-held corporation. The dilution of the stock being sold by the amount of the previously issued pre-inc stock, plus the sales commission and expenses, were simultaneously reducing the value of every quarter invested to less than 16 cents! The opinion of the writer is that it was not the intention of the sales personnel to deceive the sales subjects. However, it was gravely wrong and irresponsible of this competent, intelligent and well-seasoned staff not to report the whole truth as to what was actually happening to every dollar each investor was placing in their hands for safe-keeping.

Scores of those who purchased stock have testified to the author that they were told they were purchasing savings certificates which could be redeemed at maturity with interest. Many were surprised and raised considerable wolf-cry when they received their stock certificates, and these instruments bore legible evidence that they had bought Class A common stock, and the par value was five cents per share! This cry was partially silenced when they were advised by the company office staff that the par value was meaningless, and the book value of the stock was much higher. This could have been the perfect time for management to inform all stock purchasers of the total truth about their investment. A printed communication to all stockholders divulging the facts and advising them that this was a perfectly normal path for any company of similar mission to travel could have saved a lot of hurt and undue criticism.

It is only fair that the reader understand also that many stockholders were deeply motivated by the bargain image of the stock, at only 25 cents per share! The visionary dream of manifold returns on a small investment was too attractive to resist. Coupled with the escape hatch that even if the firm in which they placed their funds failed, they would only lose a few dollars. These people were doubtless students from the old school of hard knocks which taught them that they should never carry all their eggs in one basket. A fall (expected or not) could result in a disaster. Tragically, some members of the purchasing body were totally trusting and placed every egg they owned in an uncertain basket, doubtless trusting in the church image they were told would not let them down.

Chapter Two
Convincing Evidence

As soon as sufficient funds were amassed, the lending arm of the company was put into operation. This arm was the member of the company body that everyone was anxious to see in operation. When reached forth, it shined with the luster and brilliance of a magic wand. The time had come that tangible evidence could be presented in the form of a new church building. The city of Snellville was selected as the site for the virgin effort of the "church bank" to supply funds to erect a lovely worship facility! Like the eyes of a vast army when marching in parade and given the "eyes right" command to snap all heads and eyes in the direction of the reviewing stand, all eyes of the management and stockholders of Provident Investment Corporation were proudly focused on the targeted city!!! The evidence was prudently convincing that the mighty ship of church financing had made its maiden voyage and was now ready to test the rough seas of the huge market that anxiously awaited!

A ready market

Those who had guessed that there was an abundant church loan market were absolutely right. Doubtless, the reasons for such great demands for loans with which to

President Collins presenting a check to Rev. E. W. Bethany for the purpose of purchasing a mobile chapel.

President Collins presenting a check to Dr. B. W. Chambers. Macon, Georgia.

build churches and church-related properties, were due to such stringent requirements enforced by banking facilities. The facts remain unchanged. It is next to impossible for a small Christian group to obtain money to help advance the Kingdom of God. The same people who choose to be identified with a small gospel-promoting crowd, can drop their religious image and walk in almost any bank and obtain a personal loan. As stated previously, it is the lack of foreclosable collateral that the banker fears in loan making. Church property foreclosure is a procedure that bank officials approach with great trepidation. These fears generate a failure to process church loans, thereby creating a wealthy stockpile of the best loans in America. Hence, Provident was now able to feast upon a source that possibly would never end before the Lord Jesus returns!

The news spread rapidly around the state that a new church-lending organization was in full swing and ready to make long- and short-term loans to churches of all denominations. In a matter of a few days so many loan requests were made that it would take months to raise sufficient money to fund the first wave of requests. One parent church body alone reported that they were ready and needed to begin mission efforts in more than 25 cities, each with populations of more than 5,000. None of these towns and cities had a church affiliated with this requesting body. Many of them did not even have a full-gospel church.

The good news about the loan market surplus spurred the promoting efforts of Provident Investment Corporation, and all stoppers were pulled. The sales force was urged to plow full steam ahead and sell as much stock as possible to raise funds for a thirsty market. In a matter of a few months the 25-cent-per-share was near depletion. More than 10 million shares had been sold or bargained for. Those who were selling the stock knew, due to previous company announcements, that the next issue of stock would be selling for $1 per share.

The news of the advancing stock market price made selling a paradise. The salesmen could not write and process the order requests due to the demand. The message was loud and clear: "A few months ago a share of stock sold for five cents per share. Today you can buy a share for a measly quarter, but tomorrow you will have to pay a dollar for the same share!" The news was almost too good to be true. Scores of people were anxiously awaiting their turn to cash in on the bonanza. They were told by the sales staff that each quarter they invested would be worth one whole good ole American dollar!!! The lack of truth again came into play. However, the whole truth was not a consideration. Every available salesman was too busy filling corpulent purses with waiting funds from eager stock purchasers. The sobering words accountants call "stock dilution" were never mentioned. It is doubtful that anyone would have listened because the music being played was too sweet. Almost everyone being approached to buy appeared to be ready to march to the drummer's beat.

Greed invariably becomes a master

I doubt if anyone has ever coined the foregoing phrase used to begin this paragraph. Regardless, it is one of the most profound statements of truth ever uttered. History records the fate of the Kaisers, Hitler, Mussolini, and others who have permitted the sin of rapacity to become their master. It would be wise for those who may have rapacious aspirations to learn that none of those who sought such vanishing goals ever made it! The historical records bear out the solemn fact. The end was ruin. In view of the announced market increase, some of the salesmen hastened into the company headquarters office in Atlanta and bought huge sums of the dwindling supply of "quarter stock" (as it came to be known). They were permitted to buy this stock on signature notes with little or no down payment and no scheduled record for repayment.

The new master, of these otherwise good men, had become greed. The temptation to make some fast, easy money was too great. The scheme the enemy used to trap these respected church people is as old as the Bible itself. Adam and Eve succumbed to the Lord of Greed when they desired more than they had. Everything a man or woman could possibly need was placed in the garden, in the beginning by God himself. However, Satan was successful in helping them to see that there were other things in the garden *to be desired*. This plateau has been a painful place for mankind since the Genesis. The appetite of greed is never satisfied. As long as there are things available to be desired, Satan will be sure that Man's appentency is fed.

The disposal plan

With the supply of quarter stock depleted, the $1 offering was placed in the hands of the salesmen for marketing. The plan was very ingenious. There would be a later offering of stock, and this fourth issue was going to be sold for the handsome price of $3 per share. Armed with this foreknowledge, these salesmen were in a position to entice men from all walks of life to invest as heavily as possible. The stock being offered in a very short time was going to be worth three grand slam old American bucks for every dollar invested plus any dividends or other profits the company might earn and distribute.

To compound the wrong, some of these salesmen were also guilty of peddling and selling stock that they had previously bought for a quarter and were selling it for the going price of $1 per share or at some smaller negotiated price. None of this exorbitant profit was shared with the company but was pocketed by the seller. There may be those who shall read this treatise who will disagree with the writer as to the wrong in this matter. However, before judging too harshly, it should be stated that the matter was checked later by a securities investigator, and his opinion was that it was a criminal offense, punishable by law!

The dollar stock continued to sell fairly well as it was frequently buoyed by the promise of the $3 stock issue and the frequent financing of churches in different areas of the state. Few people have trouble in finding fault with an organization which is helping to build soul-saving stations for the betterment of mankind and at the same time gives good promise of returning a profit to its shareholders. All of these ingredients seemed to be in place, and the ship was under orders "full steam ahead!"

A drastic slowdown in stock sales was something management did not plan on. The tight money the nation was experiencing in the early to mid '70s brought an avalanche of problems for the financial world. Increasing interest rates that banks and other lending entities began to offer to attract people with money savings suddenly made the Provident Investment Corporation stock less attractive. That was coupled with the fact that the company did not disseminate financial reports of its accountability. The choice was an easy one for the prospective investor; he would place his money in institutions where it was safe and guaranteed by the FDIC. These financial debacles and a number of other problems forced the company into the need for a quick fix. I don't think Mr. Webster's dictionary nor Mr. Roget's thesaurus groups these two words for definitive purposes. Nonetheless, most of us know that a "quick fix" is something that is usually accomplished with much haste and is not intended to be permanent in the sense of repair. Some people may choose to say band-aid repair. I think either terminology is correct if one is choosing a term to define the supplemental boost or help the company management chose to use to bolster the efforts to raise funds. A number of previous commitments had been made for church loans, and these churches were in need of the promised money to construct or finish the projects already begun.

There were two courses of action taken, neither of which was prudent, due to the time element and short maturities.

The first approach was to offer short-term security notes at the very attractive interest rate of 9 percent compounded semi-annually. (Note: Most banks at this time were paying less than 7 percent on savings accounts.) These promissory notes were used in any denomination to fit the amount of funds the person had and wished to invest. From the standpoint of the investor, it was the safest security the company offered. The notes carried a first priority payoff as mandated by state securities regulations. Even though these notes may not be retired at the time of maturity, the investor was essentially guaranteed repayment by law. In the worst case scenario, the certificate would be paid ahead of all other securities.

The big problem with this effort was that short-term investments and long-term lending do not make a good marriage. The funds being taken in through this vein were due and payable in one year, and the money was being loaned for 15- to 25-year periods. Another important facet of this manner of business is that the people who have the funds to invest, in the five-figure circle, usually have the clout and ability to get the attention of outside people to show a keen interest in helping them to compel a company as respected as Provident Investment Corporation to stand up to its obligations. However, all of these securities were paid after extended renewals to very patient investors.

Financing through bond programs

Another effort that should have been ill-advised was the attempt to sell bonds to provide financing. The idea possibly would have sounded good to everyone except a good accountant. The plan was implemented whereby the people in a church group who wished to obtain loan funds would buy bonds with staggered dates of maturity. These funds were augmented by additional funds from the Provident Investment Corporation treasury to complete the loan requirements. The company (PIC) agreed to retire the bonds at maturity which was a further tightening of the noose by strangulation of short-term borrowing and long-term lending.

In a short period of time, some of these bonds began to mature, and there were not enough funds coming through the Provident Investment Corporation coffers to meet the increased demands created by the timing of the short-term investments. The situation developed to such an extent that the proverbial adage of robbing Peter to pay Paul was the standard for doing business. The reason that the "rob Peter to pay Paul" theory will not work for a lengthy period is that eventually Peter gets tired of someone holding a gun on him to take away funds to appease another party. This is not the "Win-Win" situation that most of us are accustomed to. The win-lose or the lose-win will work with some degree of tolerance if there is some measure of equality. However, the Peter-Paul plan is a sure road to disaster.

Bad news travels fast

I have never received a satisfactory answer why bad news travels so much faster than good news. One day I was waiting for a traffic light to change at a new road crossing where a bypass route crossed a major U.S. highway. The local people were not adjusted to the new stop requirements. I saw a truck loaded with hot asphalt approaching the dangerous crossing at such a speed that I knew he could not stop before bolting non-stop through the intersection. To add to the near lightning flash catastrophe, a lady – unaware of the oncoming truck – pulled out from a service store into the direct path of the loaded truck.

The driver attempted to miss the car, and the quick steerage attempt caused the top-heavy truck to flip over, and in the overturning process, the load of burning asphalt buried the car and passenger under the burning inferno. Unconsciously, I left the running pickup truck I was driving and hastened to the scene where a lady was burning to death. I snatched the driver's door open and dug the asphalt away with my bare hands and lifted the lady, whom I found out later I knew very well, and carried her to a previously summoned ambulance that was approaching the wreck scene.

I rode to the hospital in the back of the emergency vehicle at high speed with a sheriff escort. The lady was the most severely burned individual I had ever seen. The weight of the smoldering aggregate tore away strips of skin and flesh from the burning victim. I talked to her constantly on the way to the hospital to keep her from going into shock and fainting.

The hospital staff was waiting on the emergency ramp to begin treatment of the severely burned victim. The entire staff hastened in unison to relieve the suffering. However, no one bothered to check my hands or arms for burns. I also had to hitch a ride back to the north side of town where I had left a running truck.

Someone was kind enough to pull the old red Dodge pickup over to the side of the road and switch it off. I had to go home and get my wife to treat the burns. My right arm bears some scars today from the effort to save a neighbor's wife. My rewards since have been manifold, and the lady is alive today.

My point is, the news media obtained pictures of the damaged truck and car and reported the story as accurately as they knew how. My name never reached the paper. The life-saving effort was never reported, and I have never asked for recognition. However, I am confident that if I had ever been involved in the slightest scandal, my name would have hit the newspaper headline page in "second-coming type." The enigma remains the same: bad news travels a lot faster than good news!!!

The unfortunate events which developed rapidly, when the long-term lending versus the short-term borrowing collided, made news that traveled like prairie fire in a gusty wind. In a matter of days, news that Provident was in a heap of trouble, "covered Dixie like the dew." The majority of the stock that was sold was marketed in an area of about a 100-mile radius of Atlanta. The proximity of these stockholders to the Atlanta headquarters provided ideal conditions for a battleground for a group of angered shareholders against the company management team. Storms of protest were raised. The management body was helpless because the funds from the sale of stock and security notes had been loaned for long-term periods, and only a small amount was being returned each month in the form of scheduled monthly payments. There was no quick-fix for the impending dilemma.

Some of the more vocal and influential shareholders were

able to come to the company headquarters and persuaded the president under duress to refund their money or buy their stock back. However, if you were located a good distance from Atlanta, as many of us were, the news of the scandal was history before we heard about it. In hindsight, I think those who were last to hear fared somewhat better than those in the heat of battle.

Chapter Three

The Ship Runs Aground

When a company such as Provident is created, it must be nurtured until it is strong enough to travel and maneuver by itself. Time is of the essence. There of necessity must be a sufficient complement of both. No institution can be expected to return a miracle without divine intervention. Panic is the arch enemy of all organizations and institutions. It can grip a single person or a vast army and bring a deadly paralysis.

Remember when the dreaded panic enemy struck the strong nation of America in the early 1930's? There actually were no differences between financial ledgers of America the day that panic struck and the day after. The paralysis was caused by the overdemand for payment versus limited ability to pay. Consider for a moment what would happen on any given day if all of us, who have money in America's banks, were to go to the bank and demand the return of all our money. The stark truth is the banks would be unable to pay, and only those who were fortunate to be in the first wave would get their money.

Another profound truth is that almost all the money we deposit or invest in banks is put out immediately in the form of loans and other investments to return principal and interest. Whereby following this reciprocal procedure, the banks can earn a profit from the amount of interest earned from these loans. These earnings may then be used to defray the expenses of operating the bank and return interest to its investors in the form of dividends. All of these elements require time if an orderly and productive return is to be expected.

Provident Investment Corporation was organized on May 6, 1971. The minutes of a special business meeting, conducted on March 26, 1974, reflect that there was financial trouble in the company. The report of the meeting indicated that the Provident Buying Group, a wholly-owned company subsidiary, was in default and owed its parent body (Provident) more than $3,000. This albatross venture will be discussed in a later chapter. Albeit, the young company simply had not had enough time to mature sufficiently to weather the rough seas it was subjected to, coupled with the added burden of a subordinate unit losing money. The bow was now mired in the deep sands of destruction, while the stormy seas of destruction beat violently on the stern and sides!

As in all sea disasters, the captain becomes the target of wrath. Even though others may have been derelict in their demands and duties which may have contributed to the disaster, the public outcry is focused on the captain. The purpose of this idiom is neither to condemn nor justify, but to report an unbiased summary of the history of this company as accurately and authoritatively as possible. Whereby, the readers may draw their own conclusions. It is not wrong nor improper to criticize the man in charge when his decisions and actions have contributed toward a disaster of this magnitude. However, there were others who were aided and profited from the company coffers, which ultimately caused this company to strike the disastrous sands. Those who are guilty are usually able to escape the criticism and wrath of public vociferation and are usually protected due to corporate structure, while the man at the top is lashed by the tongues and pens of men!

A fiery church meeting

A number of churches were caught in the squeeze of the bond-loan arrangement. When those who had purchased bonds abruptly realized that they were holding certificates that were actually worthless pieces of paper, tempers began to flare like fireworks at a Fourth of July celebration! The company had promised to retire these bonds through funds from mortgage payments and the sale of additional stock. When the great spring of stock sales dried up, the water from the mortgage payment source was reduced to a tiny trickle!

Ironically, one of the first battlegrounds for resolution of this dilemma was in the historic area of Dalton and Chickamauga, Georgia. These great cities, where once the armies of the Confederacy faced the overpowering forces of an advancing Union (Yankee) army, became the site of one of the most violent company-church meetings ever conducted. Some of those who were there reported that the flare of tempers at the obstreperous gathering reminded them of the Yankee-Confederate confrontation in the battle of Chickamauga!

As is usually the case in most heated debates, no one

emerges a true victor. The vast Union army indeed won the battles of Chattanooga and Chickamauga, but in the midst of victory, the slain from both armies covered the battleground of the mountainous terrain. The price that we all pay in the time of struggle and violence is too great a cost to bear. Especially, when all that can be said is we won the battle. Injury to both sides is far too great a price to requite for so minor reward as personal gratification. Many times it is much wiser to permit the ego to suffer than to be assuaged.

The president suffers a nervous breakdown

Reverend Claude Collins and the headquarters staff were experiencing a constant surge of pressure from scores of investors and stockholders from almost every area of the state. This type of pressure is not ventilated easily and continues to increase like a boiling pot with a sealed lid. A favorite pastime game we used to enjoy as small boys was called "blowing the can." I feel sure our parents did not know about these very foolish experimental events. However, as children, we were not aware of the extreme danger of the fun-producing process. The experiment began with arranging some large stones in a circular fashion and placing a sealed can, half-filled with water, on the stones. Then a large fire was built around the can and heated until the can blew up. I have seen those cans rise several feet into the air and explode scattering scalding hot water over a large area! The reason for this explosion is pressure!

When a person is constantly under pressure, and there is no ventilation, the laws of nature take control, and that person will literally explode or experience a collapse of his nervous system! This was exactly what happened to the first president of this company. The fearful pressure from the apparent collapse of an institution he worked so hard to form and operate as an instrument to help advance the kingdom of God was headed for a financial debacle.

I have studied and analyzed the history of this company for a number of years. Countless hours have been spent auditing and checking. Every known accounting technique has been employed to determine exactly what caused the abrupt collapse of this corporation. I am of the candid opinion that the disaster could have been diverted if a responsible person with a good financial business background had been chosen to take the helm of the deeply troubled vessel. This person, of necessity, would need to be a miracle worker in human relations. The confidence of the people needed to be recaptured. This could have been done through sound written communication to all stockholders apprising them of the impending danger and offering a sound recovery policy. However, the entire company was seized by the spirit of fear, and a deadly paralysis held it fast!

A lesson from the pages of maritime history may serve as an aid to help the reader better understand the rescue procedures to be followed when a vessel such as Provident has run aground. First of all the "May Day" call must be given! This is the international call for help! The news of the company's encounter with disaster was kept under a tight-lip policy with little or no news being issued, while the Cinderella vessel was being beaten to pieces in a turbulent storm.

The lame captain appointed a new leader who appeared to possess all the experience and expertise to perform the miracle needed to free the company from the quicksand. The chosen successor was a young man named Cleo Jenkins who possessed a college degree in accounting and was also a certified public accountant. He was a brilliant young man with a strong Christian background. He knew the Bible like a seasoned clergyman and was able to quote more Scripture than any other person I have ever known. Every piece of correspondence bearing his signature was annotated with a verse of Scripture, including chapter and verse.

As he assumed the leadership position, he began the mammoth task of freeing the ship by himself. A lesson for all to learn, who may have aspirations to free a vessel which has run aground, is that you begin by backing up! To attempt to row forward is to court sure disaster. There are times when it is necessary for great armies to retreat, simply for the purpose of strategy planning and regrouping and reorganizing its forces. The strength of any organization is determined by how well it is able to organize and marshall its forces toward the accomplishment of its mission. The word organization comes from the word ORGANIZE! At this time Provident Investment Corporation needed the sympathy, understanding, and help of every stockholder listed in its portfolio.

It is the candid opinion of the writer that if the new president had originated correspondence to the board of directors and stockholders informing them of the impending disaster and promising a thorough study and a complete report of his findings, this measure would have bought time to repair the vessel. Maritime law dictates that the second step in recovery of a damaged ship is to repair the leaks if at all possible even if these repairs are temporary. However, a wise captain does not continue in a direction away from the harbor. It must be started in the direction of safety where others can be summoned to help with the repairs and make the vessel seaworthy again.

Apparently there was some appearance of hope that the lame vessel could continue its mission because the new captain attempted to continue on a recovery course without making the necessary repairs. There is also the element of doubt as to whether the news of costly repairs would have fallen on sympathetic ears. The logic of speculation is left for those who wish to conjure the "what if" manifest. However, the historic records of this company could be perceived in a totally different light if its records contained a document of the estimate of repairs and a sound prognosis for a course of recovery.

The glitter of cash flow

A wise old banker told me many years ago, as I was embarking on a course to hopefully achieve financial success, this old maxim, "Just because there is money in the cash register does not mean necessarily that you are making money." The people who are always carrying huge sums of cash to the bank become the envy of all of us. We are usually blinded to the fact that there are many avenues of waiting hands to absorb the apparent bonanza. No one would have difficulty in achieving business success if there were no bills to pay. However, there are always a myriad of people waiting to be paid, and many times there is not enough money to go around.

The one thing that Provident Investment Corporation had going, which was somewhat positive, was a healthy cash flow. Almost all the churches were making monthly payments on their loans, but there was a small standing army of creditors with hands stretched out and piety in their eyes. The company had a heavy burden of salaries and other overhead expenses which left little or nothing to go toward debt retirement. The average loss for the three years that Mr. Jenkins was in office exceeded $35,000 each year. And to add insult to injury, there was not a single successful income-producing idea introduced during his office tenure. There were a number of unsuccessful ideas introduced. One idea that appeared to have merit was the company's offer to assist churches in computerizing their accounting procedures. However, this idea never got off the ground due to the lack of interest and participation. The stark truth was that the vast majority of the churches were too small to buy a computer not to mention an expensive programming procedure. As time was consumed with these ideas, the hull of the ship continued to leak, and flooding became an imminent threat.

Get rich quick policy fails

The point needs to be made clear that the entire financial affairs of the corporation were lying in shambles when the successor to President Claude Collins took over. Several parcels of real estate had been purchased. All of these properties had been bought on the installment plan with high interest rates. When the stock sale funds dried up, there was not enough revenue to pay the regular overhead and retire the interest on these notes.

The company was forced to return these properties to the mortgage holders and forfeit the down payment and any other payments made in the form of principal and interest. On one particular piece of property in Alpharetta, Georgia, the company lost more than $77,000. Mr. Jenkins was able, through some equity trade-off effort, to salvage one tract of property in Gwinnett County. This tract contained 40+ acres and was the lone asset the company owned that was not debt encumbered. This property is remotely located and there appeared to be at least 10 to 15 years before the outgrowth would reach its boundaries.

All the attempts by the young president to seek an income-producing avenue was much like riding a merry-go-round. His struggles carried him round and round, up and down, leaving him at the same place he started with no new capital. Only those who have endeavored to pilot a ship with an albatross tied around their necks know the misery and disappointment of trying to keep a vessel afloat with so much damage.

The audit request that brought down the fire

At this juncture of the game, I had only been appointed to the board for a short period and was unable to lend any constructive advice due to the lack of accounting information. Numerous requests for audit reports produced nothing meaningful, and the same reply, "We do not have the money to pay for an audit," sounded like an old parrot in a pirate's den. However, I knew the real truth was that we could not afford the lack of such a vital instrument, and my final request ended in a written communication making such a demand. In the interest of economy, the board asked for financial reports prepared over the signature of the president. At this point the game of "not enough income and too much work load" came into play. This resistance was met by my personal offer to supply a young man who supervised the accounting for my business firms to help with the preparation of unofficial accounting reports. There were six sound intelligent men serving on the board at this time who were willing to help salvage the sinking vessel, but no one knew where nor how to start due to the lack of accounting information.

The offer of qualified help, without any cost to the company, was finally accepted, and the young man from my office was hastened to the company headquarters to assist in preparing operating reports and profit and loss statements for the years since the last audit report. These reports, when finished, were utterly meaningless and were a far cry from what the board had hoped to receive. The bottom line was that the company's financial status was a disaster. The three years covered by the crude report indicated that the company had lost more than $100,000! The operating capital was taken from the total loan proceeds. The sinkhole of failure had enlarged itself and was on the verge of engulfing the entire company.

A special board meeting was called to discuss the critical status of the company. At this meeting the board in unison demanded an outside audit by a reputable accounting firm even if the expenses had to be borne personally by the board members. The president elected to employ an individual accountant whose name was Doug Tilghman. It was later learned that this accountant was also a personal acquaintance of Mr. Jenkins. However, this relationship did not hinder the accounting process, and the young man began to probe the records with an indepth view. The board had hoped to get the report in a brief time, but the days became months.

Inquiries were made as to why so much time was being spent on a simple routine audit. I was informed that the accountant was having difficulty getting the needed information. Again an offer was made to provide help from my office to assist in compiling the needed data, which was respectfully declined. It was during this period that the accountant inadvertently left his brief case overnight at the office. It was on this night that someone broke into the office, seized the accountant's papers, and set the office building on fire. The investigation ruled that the fire was set by an arsonist. No one will ever know who set the office building on fire except for the person involved. One thing happened for sure. It completed the audit of the company records!

Accountant files a letter of disassociation

There is a common practice among certified public accountants to write an official communication of disassociation to the owner or other governing bodies to the effect that they are withdrawing from their audit efforts, stating the reason for their actions. This consuetude is considered very serious. Nonetheless, in compliance with the accounting requirement, this accountant/auditor wrote letters to the board of directors and Georgia Securities Investigation Department.

Upon receipt of the accountant's official letter of disassociation, my blood pressure jumped 40 points overnight! A corresponding reaction came from other directors from across the state. In a matter of a few short days, we had about the biggest political stew pot boiling you have ever seen. None of the members of the board of directors had ever had any experience in handling a matter so serious, and we were all frightened to death, jumping around like chickens with our heads cut off! In fact, there were some of us who wished we were the headless chickens!

All the ingredients to produce a big stinking stew were present and boiling profusely on the cook stove. There was the serious letter from the disgruntled accountant, several hundred dissatisfied stockholders, accountant's audit papers missing, a burned office building, essential papers missing in the fire episode, many official complaints filed with the securities department by angry stockholders, coupled with a myriad of other problems, and no money in the treasury to hire competent legal people to help put out the fire!

Investigators and law enforcement people are always eager to conduct investigations when all the suspects are in one spot, and there is nothing to do but ride over with a previously written subpoena, gather up the evidence you need, and put the suspects on notice that you will be calling for them. This case was so ripe and juicy that it attracted the attention of the chief investigator, Mr. Wallace Rogers. He made a hasty call to the burned office building and began his investigation pronto.

Ironically, Mr. Rogers lived in Albany, Georgia, where my construction company was in the process of building a sizeable church that would seat more than 5,000 people. The proximity of the construction site to the residence of the competent investigator made things easier for him. I guess you have heard the old axiom, "shooting fish in a barrel." Well, this law enforcement official had discovered a barrel full of fish, and he would almost be able to shoot them from his front porch!

As I recall, he had made previous inquiries as to the location of the directors, and after discovering that I lived in Moultrie, a city 35 miles away, and worked daily in his hometown, it doesn't take a smart man to figure out which fish he is going to draw his bead on! One Friday about mid-afternoon, the veteran investigator drove over to the job site where the huge Deliverance Temple Church was under construction. At the time I was operating a high lift-type forklift, lifting the huge fabricated timbers for the roof system of the spacious octagonal-shaped worship facility. He walked up to the noisy machine and flashed a badge that got my attention abruptly. The engine stalled as I hastened to answer the call from the distinguished lawman. I had never before had an experience of having an officer of the law flash a badge at me, but you can be sure it got my attention. My whole life has been spent as a law-abiding citizen with the exception of one minor traffic violation ticket over a 50-year period.

He was straight forward and stated his business in a manner that a first-grade school child could understand. He began his inquiry as to what I knew about the troubled state of the company of which I was a member of the board of directors. I shared the limited knowledge I had to which he responded, was the way he expected it to be. The board was indeed nothing more than a figurehead with a fancy title. The inquiry proceeded to the heart of the matter. He wanted to interrogate the accountant who had written the letter of disassociation. He informed me that the accountant was unwilling to share any information with him unless he was authorized to do so by the board of directors. He asked if I would contact each board member and ask all to attend a meeting at the Securities Investigation Department on the following Tuesday. He asked that we do this without subpoena, to which I was grateful to oblige. The brief meeting was dismissed as soon as he had my word that the board members would be present. I can recall only twice in my lifetime when fear so gripped my body that my knees smote together like the dead bones in Ezekiel's graveyard. Once was when returning from Hilo, Hawaii, and attempting a landing in a C-46 cargo type aircraft at Hickam Air Force Base in Hawaii. We overshot the runway and nearly crashed into a loaded fuel tanker truck before getting the plane back into the air. I shook with such fear that I could not keep the ear phones on my head while my knees played "Yankee Doodle Dandy." Oh, you guessed it, the second time was when Mr. Wallace Rogers flashed his badge at a Holiness preacher, who had never been so close to a lawman's authority symbol before!

Contact with the other board members instilled the same fear in them that I had experienced. Never before had there been a group of Bible-believing men who knew so little about what we were being called upon to talk about. I had never been in a courthouse before except to buy a car tag, and suddenly I found myself on my way to a high level meeting one block west of the gold-domed capitol building in Atlanta, Georgia. I had always wanted to go to the building where the governor's office is, but this trip was not the way I wanted to begin high level meetings!

Chapter Four

Big-Time Investigation
vs.
Small-Time Suspects

The famous old cliche "innocent until proven guilty" uttered frequently in legal halls does not provide all the liberty that is implied. The investigative process is usually lengthy, and the words "personal privacy" are vernacular with a meaningless sound. Innocent or guilty, the probing process is embarrassing and painful.

These thoughts and a legion of others clouded my mind as I drove down the off-ramp marked "State Capitol." I had only viewed this historic structure with a passing glance. As a child, I had wondered if I would ever roam its halls, possibly catch a glimpse of the famous people who worked there. However, as I walked past the huge marble and granite structure, I was so uncomfortable and frightened that I only gave a glance in passing with a firm promise that one day soon I would return and do the things I had dreamed about in the days of my childhood. For now I hastened my stride in the direction of the huge governmental building that housed the Securities Investigation Department. I was somewhat relieved when I arrived and found the entrance foyer marked "Secretary of State." That surely sounded a lot better than

"Investigation Department."

As I walked into the lavish foyer, standing in the hall were all of the familiar faces of the people I had talked to a few days before on the telephone. A quick search of each face revealed that they were as frightened as I was. However, there is some solace in company, and my fears somewhat subsided as I looked into the sympathetic eyes of each board member and gave him a hearty handshake. They gathered around me, and I told them jestingly, "I guess we will all hang together!"

Taking a few minutes to enjoy the comfort of renewing our friendship, I walked over to the elevator and pushed the button where the arrow pointed up. The most comforting thing I knew about the meeting we were scheduled to attend was that it was in the upward position. The elevator stopped with a soft ring of the bell, and six anxious men crowded aboard as I pushed the button marked four. The elevator hastened upward, and with another small ring, the control light flashed four. As the doors slid open, all passengers walked toward a large open door where the somewhat familiar face of Mr. Wallace Rogers could be seen. He arose and came through the doors and greeted us in a very cordial manner. For the first time I could sense a fibre of friendship emanating from the man whom I knew could be as tough in his mannerism as J. Edgar Hoover!

The large conference room was somewhat littered with voluminous piles of records bearing a distinct odor of having been burned and exposed to tremendous heat. I recognized the records as being those that had escaped destruction by the attempt of an unknown arsonist. It was clear that the charred matter had been searched thoroughly by the security investigators to glean every ounce of evidence. It was obvious that the keen investigative minds had gathered enough valuable information to let them know what transactions had taken place within the walls of a very private office.

As each board member was seated, without regard to protocol, he was introduced to the accountant, who had fired the warning shot that there was trouble in the camp. He appeared to be as uncomfortable as those shaking his hand for the first time and taking a seat around the large octagonal shaped conference table. After all were seated, a fearful quietness momentarily occupied the room. This silence was hastily broken by the chief investigator who stated the purpose of the meeting, moving slowly from one person to another establishing rigid eye contact. The message was loud and clear. He wanted to direct a truckload of questions at the auditing accountant, and he wanted the permission of the board members to accomplish this mission. He hopefully would be able to gather information from this source and blend it with the data gathered from the partially burned records and other sources he had tapped prior to this meeting.

A quick elevator to the top

The tenor of the meeting quickly dictated the need for interim leadership. The meeting was momentarily halted by board member Frank Page who suggested the wisdom in appointing a person to act as board chairman for the crucial gathering.

Very quickly, board member Dr. G. Herfin Taylor

placed his hand on my shoulder with a firm grip and said in his usual firm and polite manner, "I nominate this young man to take this position, since he has been in on all of the investigation procedure so far." A quick response of hands gave the unison sign that the interim board chairman and president would be Shelvie Summerlin. I learned for the first time in my life how it felt to be in charge of a building on fire and not one fire bucket to gather water to fight the blazing flame! The term "Mr. President" seemed a trite phrase as the meeting resumed its investigative focus.

Board member Jonathan Ostrom very wisely made the first resolution by reserving privilege to halt the meeting at any time when we felt the information being obtained could be considered incriminating and in need of special legal input. The resolution passed unanimously and received the nodded approval of the eager investigator.

The second resolution was made by member Dewey T. Bryson. The motion would authorize Mr. Doug Tilghman, a certified public accountant who had been retained to perform an accounting audit of Provident Investment Corporation, to divulge information to the state of Georgia obtained during the audit process which could aid the securities department in performing a thorough investigation of the practices of company personnel. The motion followed the *Roberts Rules of Order* format and also received unanimous approval.

The meeting returned to its tense question and answer forum after the brief parliamentary recess. Mr. Rogers resumed his orbiting mannerism with a smooth parlance by asking each board member if he knew the company had been raped. The strong vernacular quickly engaged all minds as to the severity with which this man was approaching his evidence-gathering strategy. He continued with convincing oratory that the case was considered very serious and that the company had been rapaciously treated by the incumbent leadership. This suggested indictment extended to all members of the leadership body, including the board members whose ears were hearing the strong language from a veteran investigator. Even though not a single board member had received one cent of compensation for numerous trips to Atlanta for meetings with company business significance nor salaries, we clearly and fearfully understood that we could be held liable for the unwise, unlawful acts of others. I suddenly felt a drop in my abdomen section and a surge in my blood pressure by a heart that raced to supply the needed blood to keep my head clear and combat the induced fear. I became abruptly aware of the unannounced liability I had incurred a few years before when I was elected as a member of the board of directors. I, along with five other men, could be held accountable for the actions of others even though there was not one stitch of evidence to indicate that any member of this board had done nor contributed to the doing of anything illegal or immoral.

The seasoned investigator continued by laying volumes of convincing evidence before the small awestruck audience. The questions directed to the accountant and his responses supplied hair-raising fuel to a group of men who were already overly flabbergasted with the revelation received from the orbicular investigator. The accountant obviously approved of the harsh criticism being heaped upon a man who was to have an opportunity to respond to the accusation at a later date.

The strongest charge came as a result of large salaries being paid to members of the office staff as opposed to lack of inducing a revenue-producing return. The Ironside image the investigator developed as he moved into this matter caused his face to redden with anger. He hastened the pace to gain the support from the body present that they should join him in condemnation of the numerous irresponsible acts that were committed to divest the innocent company of its few remaining assets.

At one juncture of the accusational tirade, he raised his fist to pound on the conference table to emphasize the point that the stockholders of any company had a right to expect a fair return for salaries paid; especially from a man with a college degree in accounting and with the unique ability to successfully pass a CPA exam! I thought the fiery indictment should be good medicine for any person who receives a salary for services performed and willfully should expect to compensate those who fund their livelihood with goods or services commensurate with the amount received. This had certainly not been the case as the incomplete audit report bore good testimony.

Public trust is an awesome trust to betray, and when there is compelling evidence to substantiate such a claim, there will always be an army of those who will join ranks and lash out their fury upon the guilty suspect. As stated before, this treatise is intended to neither justify nor condemn but to present a factual and orderly dialogue. It is the firm hope of the writer that those eyes which read this report from this point of observation will be reminded of the sacredness of being placed in positions of public and private trust. Even though it may be embarrassing and humiliating when there is a breach of trust, it is not unfair for the betrayed to return a fair response for their hurt. This observation is made from the premise that there were people from all walks of life who bought stock in this company with the greatest respect for those who marketed the securities and believed in the mission the company was designed to follow. It was indeed a sacred trust to take hard earned money that in most cases had been painfully saved and invest these funds with the idea that they would be used to build churches and advance the kingdom of God. For these funds to be dissipated through non-compensatory means is a sure way to court disaster and incur the wrath of those who have dared to trust you!

The addendum that stopped the clock

Corporate authority is established by the legislative bodies of most all states and territorial ruling agencies. The right to establish entities to function within the guidelines of these provisions is the right of every American who may aspire to do business through the corporate structure. Albeit, it is not a license to conduct these affairs in any manner other than professional. The annals of historical archives are filled with firm attestation of the plight of those who have chosen to do otherwise. A person may create a lawful corporate body, own all its stock, conduct affairs in any manner desired, but there is always the immutable truth: there is only the right way and the wrong way. Either way may be chosen. If there is no watchdog nor accountability, there is no one to accuse, consequently the company's history will pass without notice. The case in this dissertation was different in that it had applicable constitution and bylaws that required accountability, even though the operative accounting network was closely held.

The now red-faced investigator continued his trail of evidence seeking like a hound dog on a hot trail. He noted that there was an abrupt mental collapse of the original chief executive officer, and also a hastened change in the managerial status. However, there were ample guidelines in effect for the succeeding party to follow, and these guidelines should have been followed or officially changed by the new governing body. This was not the case, retorted the apparently angry lawman. He surmised the incumbent as being a man that wrote his own rules, called all the shots, and acted as a lone ranger in running a company that he had little to no financial interest in!

At this point the impassioned man began to sound like a Harvard-trained lawyer making a veritable pitch to a sympathetic jury for a sound conviction of the accused to whom all the accusations were being directed. There were numerous expenditures which were considered personal and salaries which were in excess of the amount approved by board authority. Apparently sensing a need for verification of his conjectured approach, he turned and focused sharply on the nearby accountant and asked him to share his findings and opinions regarding the expenditures of the company by the incumbent management.

Nervously reaching for his neatly prepared notes, he turned a page and began by stating that he had been asked to do the audit apparently because of a lengthy friendship with the incumbent president. An agreement was reached, and the audit began on a very friendly note but developed a very serious discord when he began to question many of the expenditures and requested authorization for somewhat inappropriate fiscal accountability. The auditing process reached an impasse when he asked for specific authority for payment of back salaries to the president from funds when a church had elected to pay off its loan in full, by virtue of a refinancing arrangement with another firm. He stated that he was told that Cleo (name of incumbent president) was promised $25,000 annually plus travel expenses to run the company. When asked for the specific authority, he was furnished an addendum to company minutes where a salary of like amount was approved.

At this point of the meeting, the eyes of the board members began to quickly shift from one to the other as to inquire where and when such an action took place. Mr. Rogers, instinctively sensing the lack of knowledge, interrupted the accountant's report and asked how many members of the board knew about the meeting where a salary of $25,000 annually was approved for the president. A head-shaking silence revealed that no one had any knowledge of such a meeting nor subsequent meeting where an addendum was approved to establish a salary of such an amount, especially a company as financially troubled as the one in question. Sliding back in his chair, the obviously disgusted investigator asked the young accountant to resume his account of the ill-fated audit.

Patently aware that the remarks he was making could be faced again, possibly in a court of law, the accountant resumed by stating how patiently he had told his friend about the trail of expenditures as opposed to sparse income. He stated that he was informed that considerable effort had been made to induce income, but that all confidence had been lost in the company, and no one was willing to invest in a firm as hopelessly lost as Provident.

The meeting shifted back and forth from accountant to investigator with a barrage of questions and answers and none apparently to the tasting of the information-gathering interrogator. After more than three hours, which seemed like days, Mr. Rogers indicated that he was finished with the questioning of the accountant and board members and that they were free to go. Loaded with enough explosive information to blast the city of Atlanta from the face of the map, the meeting adjourned without proper parliamentary procedure, but no one in the crowd dared to rise to a point of order and request a proper ending according to *Robert's Rules of Order!*

The elevator was summoned for the trip down hill, and each member of the board filed into the chamber of a quiet machine which was doubtless the pride of the Otis Elevator Company. I don't remember who pushed the button to start us down hill, but it appeared that we were going to continue this downward ride a long time after the elevator stopped!

Chapter Five

The Painful Process of Changing the Guard

The meeting held near the state capitol building erased all doubt that the guard must be changed. A brief assembly in the foyer by the board of directors gave complete authority to the newly-elected president and vice president Jonathan Ostrom to travel immediately to Gainesville, Georgia, where the temporary headquarters was located. The plan was to locate the bank where the company funds were entrusted. These funds were to be frozen together with any other company assets consigned to the bank.

A visit to the first bank located by the dismayed twosome was a lucky strike. We cautiously approached a very pleasant secretary seated near a large banking office and asked to see the chief banking officer. That both of us were dressed in the best attire we possessed had apparently impressed the young lady that our business was serious. She immediately arose and ushered us into the office of the bank president. A very impressionable man in his mid-40's arose from behind a large mahogany desk to greet us. Names were pleasantly exchanged, and the purpose of our visit was stated. The graying banking official listened intently, flashing searching eyes from one visitor to the other as the disastrous story unfolded of a company created and designed for high and noble purposes, now stripped of almost every meaningful asset it possessed.

Sensing the sincerity of the two strangers seated in his office, he interrupted the step-by-step story and asked what action we wished the bank to take to intercede in the serious matter. The hasty plan approved by the board earlier was presented.

1. Freeze all bank accounts.
2. Establish a funds withdrawal plan.
3. Relieve all company employees.
4. Transfer all funds and assets to another banking institution, to be named later.

These requests obviously appeared to be proper and reasonable because the sympathetic banker quickly wheeled the large executive chair over to the side of his desk to the desk-mounted computer screen and began punching in characters and figures. The obedient machine quickly obeyed every command from the fingers of the competent master and graphically displayed the requested summary. A somewhat faint look came upon the face of the accommodating officer as he turned the face of the computer screen in the direction of his guests. He motioned for us to step closer to the screen and read the results. My first impression was there must be a banking error. It did not seem possible that the remaining banking balance of a corporation that had been entrusted with the savings and investments of others amounting to more than $2 million, was less than $2! In fact, the checking account balance was $1.56! Coupled with this frightening revelation, we were further informed that the company we had come to rescue had no other assets, pledged or unpledged, in the safekeeping of the Gainesville banking institution.

While the two troubled company officers remained standing before the truth-bearing computer screen, the silence caused by the startling report was broken as the banker asked what we wanted to do with the dismal residue of company cash flow. Not waiting for a response from my dear friend who stood close by in a near state of shock, I asked the officer to cut us a check for the amount of the remaining balance. Armed with a check representing the total purchasing power of Provident Investment Corporation, two men vividly aware of the awesome responsibilities which lay ahead, walked out of the respected banking institution with less than enough money to buy two hamburgers at the McDonald's restaurant which could be seen from the bank's portico! I jestingly asked Jonathan if he would make up the difference and I would buy the drinks. Thusly, we would deplete the total cash liquidity of the firm we represented. He declined my offer!

A trip up the mountain

A number of shrewd maneuvers by my predecessor had enabled him to purchase Wauka mountain, a majestic site, which was situated a few miles north of Clermont, on U.S. Highway 129. It was here on this sprawling landscape that he had elected to move the company headquarters. This arbitrary decision was reached in lone ranger style without the knowledge of any member of the board of directors. The fire in the former office building on Shallowford Road in Atlanta necessitated a move, but no one had an idea that we would climb the summit so quickly!

I lifted a road atlas from the backseat of my car and placed it on the hood for easy viewing. A finger was placed on the well-marked spot where Gainesville was located, a quick trip northward with the finger located the historic mountain. We were to learn later that Indians had lived on this baronial land since a time known only to God. Some influential member of the prehistoric tribe had decided that the hallowed grounds should be called Wauka Mountain. With the next destination stop clearly in focus, we boarded the Impala Chevrolet automobile and sped off in the direction of a famous mountain marked by a small dot on the road map.

In a matter of a few minutes, we were entering the small town of Clermont, in sight of the butte-shaped mountain. The Blue Ridge Mountains were well defined in the background forming a site too marvelous to describe with words. As we made the left turn into the road leading to Wauka Mountain, I thought how unfortunate we were not to have something as pleasant to discuss as the tranquil setting of the rolling hills and mountains that lay before us. A small building on the left was easily identifiable as the office that housed the remaining records of the near defunct organization. The only thing remaining with a remote possibility of being solvent was the name Provident. The name means "making provisions for the future." However, the day when this royal vessel would sail again, attempting to fulfill its mission, was in the distant future and there was much doubt if she would ever sail again.

The sound of the automobile tires rolling in the graveled yard sent a message indoors that hastily brought a troubled looking person named Cleo Jenkins from inside. The distraught appearance was strongly supported by a holster-laden revolver strapped tightly around his waist. An apology was the first thing he offered for the visibly displayed weapon. He stated that he had been fearful of intruders and also that he had used the side arm to shoot some beavers that were menacing a beautiful lake which lay in the foreground. Neither Jon nor I felt any fear of the weapon-laden person; however, he obviously was a victim of fear and depression. The three of us had been friends for several months, but a friendship between Cleo and Jon predated our relationship by a considerable time frame.

The conversation quickly shifted from the uneasy pace set by the presence of a troubled friend to a far more serious note, the unpleasant task of changing the guard. The change was absolutely necessary or the entire board could be held personally liable for the continued pattern of abuse and improper management. I have never asked Jon how he felt about that dark hour when two friends were compelled by law to relieve another friend of his duties and advise him that he possibly could be indicted for criminal negligence. My thoughts focused on the Old Testament account about Saul, Jonathan, and David. The reigns of leadership were stripped from Saul a long time before he fell so tragically before the sword of man. Our friend had been divested of his management right the day before in the conference room of the Secretary of State's office building. An avalanche of charges of abuse and improper management policies were heaped upon him by a highly respected professional investigator and an accountant friend who dared to release his firm convictions even though it could possibly mean the toppling of a friend from a highly respected position and set the tone for possible incrimination.

We entered the office building and were seated very casually around the large executive type desk. A high back upholstered chair was part of the office furniture that had been selected to add class to the prestigious office. This chair was set in back of the desk; however, the man upon whom rested the honor of occupying that chair did not take his place as usual in other meetings but sat on the corner of the desk exhibiting worry and anxiety. The silence was broken as I began by informing Cleo of the very serious charges leveled against him at the Securities Investigation Department by able investigators who were determined to present sound basis for his dismissal from office and the mountain of evidence that could lead at least to a lengthy court process and possible convictions. Jon and I both noticed that revealing such a great volume of evidence against our friend enhanced his fears and frustration.

The straw that broke the camel's back

The room atmosphere shifted into a higher frame of fear as I asked Cleo if he remembered the addendum to the minutes where the executive board was supposed to have authorized a salary for him amounting to $25,000 per year. He nodded that he was aware of the instrument.

I continued by informing him that the real problem was that none of the directors was aware of having authorized such inappropriate action nor were they willing to support such a move at this time. The small check I held in my pocket amounting to $1.56 was conclusive proof of the absurd claim. The real truth was that it was no more than hope which he had imposed upon himself, and no one in the ranks of directorship of Provident was going to support any salary adjustment.

Cleo finally responded by stating that the former president Claude Collins had authorized the salary to entice him to take over the company. However, I had already checked this matter with Collins, and he categorically denied any knowledge of agreeing to such a ridiculous increase. Collins also added that he thought Jenkins was to get a salary of $8400 per year, the same that he was getting plus a travel allowance. He was willing to testify in a court of law to this effect. I didn't bother sharing this information at this time, for I could readily discern that the basis of the claim for the addendum was completely unfounded. The stark truth was no salary basis was established for Jenkins other than a personal claim. He thought $25,000 per year was not ample compensation for an accountant of his caliber. No one was willing to debate this point. However, anyone with a third-grade education should have known in the beginning that a lame duck company like Provident could not support any meaningful salaries. The salary of $25,000 yearly for the president, $9,000 per year for the secretary plus travel allowances for both was nothing more than sand castles in the sand that would soon be washed away with the rising tide.

I made mention of some financial statements prepared by Jenkins and an employee from my company. Even though these reports were a distant cry from what was expected, there were a number of meaningful entries that reflected claims against Provident from the incumbent president. One of these claims which was absolutely absurd, was a claim for back salaries amounting to several thousand dollars. This figure was assumed to represent the difference between the amounts the company had already paid and what it was unable to pay, due to the lack of cash flow. Unfortunately for the company, a few months before the collapse of its financial structure, a church in Valdosta was asked by Jenkins to pay off its mortgage combination of bonds and moneys from other sources. The pastor of the church, who is now a member of the board of directors, later informed us that he was advised that the company was in a severe financial bind and needed the lump sum payoff to keep it afloat.

An arrangement to refinance the mortgage was made hastily, and the church was able to issue a check for an amount in excess of $50,000 to pay off the mortgage. Tragically, Jenkins issued himself a check for $25,000 to retire part of the claim for back salaries he had filed against the company. We were to learn later that he had used this money to arrange a financial deal with a Gainesville bank which enabled him to gain control of Wauka Mountain.

A previous owner had defaulted on a loan to buy and

develop the historic site into a combination of residential homes and pleasure resorts, including an exclusive golf course. The potential of this gorgeous landscape held a glamour for the young president that he could not resist. The solemn truth was actually that he nor the company was able to make such a giant financial step even though a step-by-step miracle and geniuses were needed to save the deeply troubled company. The prospects of Wauka Mountain becoming a bonanza appeared to have considerable merit, but Cleo Jenkins nor Provident was able to give the financial help needed to bring the bonanza into existence. Sadly, there was never an offer from the man who had led the company for a few years to make Provident a partner in a venture he felt was a gold mine that he expected to return exorbitant amounts of profit. Even if an offer had been made, the wisdom of the two members of the board of directors, standing in the office at Wauka Mountain resort office, would have compelled them to decline. A banking balance of less than $2 was a far-flung amount from the enormous sum needed to fulfill the dreams of a successful resort area coupled with comfortable homes nestled among the numerous sites afforded by the silent mountain, which had been the benefactor for a $25,000 down payment from the coffers of a troubled financial institution.

The dreams and possibilities of the mountain doubtless occupied the minds of all present in the rustic office. Albeit, there were two men present who were not about to begin chasing rainbows and sand castles which were certain to add to the misery and hasten the fate of a company they were sworn to defend and support. Cognizant of this solemn responsibility, I broke the moment of silence and advised Jenkins that the board had unanimously voted to relieve him of his duties and that imminent arrangements were in progress to move the company headquarters to Moultrie, Georgia, before any recovery attempts were made.

Verbal agreements were reached to effect the transfer of the headquarters of a financial institution, which a few months earlier was considered to be sound and strong; but this day it appeared destined to failure and ruin. Arrangements were made for a truck to pick up the records and files and the meager remaining inventory of office furniture which had survived the unexplained fire and the move from the old office on Shallowford Road to the Wauka Mountain resort.

In a matter of a few days, the total assets of a once dream corporation lay scattered over the floor area of a borrowed office, and no one was sure where to start, attempting to reassemble the pieces of a scattered puzzle. It was obvious from the outset that the process was going to be frustrating and difficult. There was a mountain of evidence which indicated that a number of the pieces to the puzzle were missing and the best to be hoped for was an incomplete picture.

The writer was determined to do the best possible job of putting the broken pieces together even if a complete story was unattainable. His patience and skills were to be tried under the heavy pressure of the hammer and anvil. Buoyed by the knowledge that there were many people that he had knowledge of, who had placed their meager savings in a company which had proven to be an unkind steward, and he was determined to at least give a responsible accounting of the debacle. The road ahead was to be rough and bumpy, but when one is driven in search of truth if the hunger is deep enough, cost and person and comfort are of minor consideration.

Chapter Six

Rise Again

As a child, I saw a portrait on a book cover of a man with his arms locked around his wife as they observed the ash burning inferno of what remained of their home. I didn't need to read the book; the whole story lay in torrid form, written all over the faces of the young couple.

Some of the burning ashes represented the crib and charred body of a baby that was left asleep, while husband and wife labored in a nearby field to earn a livelihood. No one could point a finger of neglect, since the mother frequently made hasty trips to peek in on the gift from above. Chapter after chapter was written on the tanned faces of the dear couple. However, in the absence of neighbors and friends who were doubtless miles away, the author of the book penned these words below the heart-rending picture – WE SHALL RISE AGAIN!!!

When people agree on anything being done, the job is essentially complete. The gospel writer, Matthew, offered the foundational formula for success, quoted from the lips of the Master, "Again I say unto you, that if two of you shall agree on earth as touching any thing that they shall ask, it shall be done for them of my Father which is in heaven" Matthew 18:19. This promise is not bounded on any other conditional premise than AGREE!

We are extremely fortunate that there were not more financial obligations; because financial conditions could not have been at a lower ebb. Any possible financial help for the monumental task of resurrecting the company must come through members of the board of directors. Any help received, of necessity, would be on a loan basis.

There is an old Southern cliche which says, "One good thing about being on the bottom is there is but one way to go." I am not ready to admit that this counsel is totally true, for the new management team was to find out there are two ways, deeper and up! However, sound fiscal principles were installed to guarantee that the descent was minimal.

Free office rent provided

The timing of the move from Clermont to Moultrie, even though tragic, could not have been at a better time. The writer had made firm plans several months before to retire in 1981. The timing was going to coincide with the completion of a mammoth construction project in Albany, Georgia, by my construction company. The office this firm occupied in Moultrie was owned by me, and the workload had already begun to subside. There was ample space in the building to house the records of both firms. An offer to the use of the building with no rent nor utility charge was graciously accepted by the board. In fact at this point there was no revenue to offset any expenses, and there were a number of unknown costs which everyone expected to surface.

There would be no change in personnel, since the duty of operating the company was to be assumed by the newly-elected president. This service, too, was provided without cost to the company. The only regular expense incurred was the installation of a telephone and the regular monthly billing. This tight ship policy was implemented with the hope and prayer that the few remaining monthly church mortgage payments would be allowed to accumulate for many of the numerous expenses which were to come shortly.

All salaries frozen

The previous administration had arbitrarily established a salary of $25,000 per year for the president and $9,000 for the secretary plus a liberal allowance for auto and travel expenses. The total income from all sources was not adequate to defray all these expenses. In an effort to combat the shortfall, the former president accumulated the deficit in the forms of "back salaries due." No one is sure where nor when he expected to recoup this deficit, other than possibly another one of the existing church loans would pay off early in a lump sum payment. This did occur earlier, as alluded to in an earlier chapter where $50,000 was paid with reticence. The idea would have been very clever if time had permitted development, even though it would have been extremely difficult for anyone to justify a salary of that magnitude in return for nothing profitable for the company's coffers.

There was never a commitment made to any board member or committee to compensate them for their services in the form of "back salaries." The name of the game was survival, and no one was able to see beyond the whirlpools of a sinking vessel.

The zero salary and near zero expense policy was sufficient to stabilize the company and buy some time to repair the many injuries. This was going to require a considerable time frame and money. Ironically, money was not the primary concern, for there was an abundance of sweat and labor, and this treasured asset was going to be given by a number of people. Even though the cash register did not ring each time this gracious commodity was donated, each hour of time became a current asset in the form of savings. The new president and board of directors paid all their personal and travel expenses for several months. Not one time during this crucial period was there one note of complaining nor a desire expressed for compensation at a later date. Everyone was more concerned with getting the vessel repaired, where she could once again reach forth a strong lending hand to a multitude of needy churches.

Now where do we stand?

The merchant can close the doors of his business at the end of any business day, count the money in his cash register, inventory the goods on hand, make a few other accounting adjustments, and determine exactly where he stands financially. However, there were a number of other matters that needed to be investigated and verified before any real meaningful accounting reports could be prepared.

Eager to establish this basis, good or bad, the new president contacted a local accounting firm and asked about the possibility of their help to make this determination. Mr. William O. (Bill) Pifer, the owner and chief officer of the firm, was contacted and reluctantly agreed to help with this matter. No firm price was quoted, but he estimated that a minimum cost of $3,000 would be required, and the charge could possibly run much higher. Now this may not seem like a lot of money to some folks, but to a fellow who is working for nothing and the money barrel is empty, it's a little more than Monday morning lunch money!

Agreement was reached with Mr. Pifer, and he immediately began the mountainous task of searching the records that had survived the fire in an attempt to prepare a meaningful financial report. The first thing he discovered was serious enough to ring the bell for a three-alarm fire!

<u>No financial statements nor federal and state income taxes had been filed in three years</u>.

That's enough to curl an Irishman's moustache! This discovery was one of the greatest enigmas of the entire fiasco. How any persons with the skills and intellect of the previous office staff could evade the preparation of these necessary documents is beyond words. This ill-advised policy was to court disaster and invite the early intervention of the federal agencies into a volatile matter that was already on the verge of explosion!

Needless to say, stomachs began to churn and blood pressures began to rise when this information was shared with the board of directors. The situation could not have been worse than to have seized a live 10-foot alligator by the tail and be expected to hold on! However, I am told that the only place with any measure of safety around a big live alligator is to hold onto the tail until somebody arrives to help tie his mouth shut! I am not ready to approve nor deny any of this alligator theory, but I can assure you that I was determined to hold on until help arrived!

At this point no one knew how much money in the form of penalties and taxes would be due on the state tax return due to the amount of securities (stock) the company owned. The wisdom of the wise old accountant, who was patiently and thoroughly working on the necessary documents to reveal this figure, assured me it would be a few thousand dollars. At this juncture, I did the only sane and prudent thing I could do by going to the nearby drugstore and buying five giant sized bottles of Pepto Bismol! A good friend came into the office a few days afterward and noticed the large inventory of stomach tranquilizers. He jestingly asked who had the upset stomach? I told him that the five bottles represented less than one bottle apiece for seven members of the board of directors, who were possibly going to need a whole lot more before the storm subsided!

Only a few agonies equal the task of preparing an accounting history for a three-year period where every cent of income was spent and the hole being dug was getting deeper with each expenditure. The attitude of the previous managing body seemed to have been if there was money in the cash register, it was o.k. to spend it. The practice was a close kinsman to an old story I heard a few years ago about two brothers back in the 1930 era, in a local area of South Georgia. (You probably heard it happened in Alabama.) But a farmer told me the other day that it absolutely occurred in South Georgia, for they were his distant cousins!

Regardless, the story I heard indicated that the young

brothers were not overly endowed with intelligence and only a smidgen of education. They decided to try their hand in the American free enterprise system by buying and selling watermelons.

They owned a small pickup truck with some improvised side bodies, designed to increase the load capacity of the truck. They drove to the local farmers' market and found another farmer with a load of the red meated delicacies and engaged him in the usual buy-sell agreement. A price of 50 cents per watermelon was agreed upon and buyers and seller loaded the small truck to capacity with 50 of the streaked, elongated farm-grown beauties. Each one was loaded with an investigative thump, which met the criteria of the buyers. The farmer was paid the sum of $25, and the young business men shuttled out of the market place on their way to Atlanta to sell the load of produce for a fortune of hope.

During the trip they determined that they wished to be volume dealers. Therefore, a strategy of low-pricing was agreed upon to help them accomplish the established objective. They would sell the watermelons for 25 cents each!

The strategy worked and in a matter of a few minutes after arriving in Atlanta, they had sold all their watermelons.

On the way home, the brother who was charged with the financial custody began to count the silver coins. As the second count was finished, he suspected that they had not made any money, so he broke the news to the driver brother who was fastidiously attending to the driving duties. He pondered the matter in a few moments of silence and replied to his brother that the only thing he could figure out was that they should buy a bigger truck!

Now, no one had to be a Harvard lawyer to figure out that this company did not need a bigger truck! Especially, with the deficit spending amounting to more than $30,000 per year and no apparent hope of increasing the income to offset the disastrous course the company was on. A sound policy to increase the income was desperately needed. The viable alternatives to help accomplish this were limited, but a determination was made to vigorously pursue every avenue of hope, even while the investigative accounting process was in progress.

Swap and trade

Take a look at those two nouns I have chosen to begin this paragraph, SWAP AND TRADE! These words have enabled a multitude of folks to do business even in the absence of American greenbacks and valuable coins. Even in times when currency is scarce, there is usually an abundance of sound commodities which are available to help industrious folks traffic and trade.

The company was literally strapped due to the lack of cash flow; however, it was determined that we did own some shares in a land syndicate deal in Henry County. The manner through which the company came to own these shares is another humdinger deal that added some gray hairs and a few pepto attacks to each board member. As I understood the clever scheme, a total of 20 shares were sold to individuals at the price of $3500 per share. This gymnastic move was made (mind you totally legal) to purchase a small track of land near Ellenwood in Henry County. The land purchase was handled through a syndicate, known as the Henry County Venture. The company was not involved in any way in this venture; however, the former president came into possession of three shares of this land speculation effort. This development apparently transpired prior to his tenure as the chief operating officer.

Remember the addendum in chapter four that brought on the fireworks display? This addendum was designed to grant authority for a fixed salary and also to purchase the three shares Jenkins owned, for a price of $10,500. This sale and transfer was effected without the knowledge or approval of the board. The payments were made from the operating fund that was almost as dry as the proverbial wood chip. Albeit, the troubled company owned an asset that there was no cash market for and carried a value considerably less than the purchased price. There was one positive side to this fiasco. Here was an asset of at least some value, and since there was no ready market, it had a good chance in remaining in the custody of the company.

One of the board members, who could not resist the temptation of the Henry County bonanza, personally bought several shares. He was mired in the gummy clay of the land deal and was on a footing comparable to where the company was positioned. There was also another land deal similar to the Henry County venture in Brazelton where the company and Jon Ostrom had been cajoled into another share purchase arrangement. The properties were valuable due to location, but the downside was the immutable fact that the possibility of sale and development was a few too many years away. Mr. Jenkins was mindful of this stubborn fact as his efforts to sell or move the properties had been fruitless. Caught in the middle of a pressure debacle between the friendship of a trusted friend and pressure from a failing company, he presented a swap-trade proposition to the board. Since both company and board members owned near equal interest in each land venture, a proposal was made to swap these interests; thereby giving each complete ownership of a piece of real estate. The board agreed to this arrangement and approved the trade arrangement, resulting in Provident being the major owner of the Henry County venture.

The words syndicate, venture, limited partnership and others were all foreign words to my vocabulary. But the able guiding hand of a very wise attorney, Mr. Charles Alford Jr., steered the company on a course, even though rough and bumpy, proved to be safe and eventually profitable. The process was a master teacher with a firm rod for correction, but the lessons to be learned were never to be forgotten. They would serve in the years to come as a reminder, that while land deals and bonanza speculations are wise and prudent paths for some to follow, others should walk in great trepidation! However, a company with a dead albatross hanging around its neck would not be a participant unless it was affordable and possibly could serve a good purpose to help advance the kingdom of God.

Making a deal work

The writer was privileged to have an intimate friend who was president of a bank in the small town where he had lived most of his life. Frequently during visits, this banker would impart nuggets of golden wisdom to his young friend, who was one of the area's leading building contractors. My business included residential and commercial building. In order to keep full-time employment for several craftsmen and laborers, it was necessary to do a considerable amount of speculative building. The term speculative meaning to build buildings without a ready buyer but hoping to secure one before or soon after completion of the building. It was during the early stages of this building venture that one of the golden nuggets of wisdom, passed out by my banker friend, came to be very beneficial. The wisdom Mr. Paulk Reeves shared was, "You can sell anything to anybody if that person has a need and you can handle all the arrangements."

Although I was not absolutely sure what the correct meaning of the terminology, "all the arrangements" was, I had at least part of the solution. I had *anything*, the other two parts of the "anybody and arrangements" remained an enigma! However, before long, after turning the puzzle pieces in many directions, they began to fit.

I soon learned that if my prospect liked my product and was short of each, (which incidentally, is the reason why most deals don't work) that I could provide a little financing for the down payment, and the prospect became a buyer. In reality what I was providing was self-financing of a portion of the profit. This idea from my friend did wonders for our business. The initially small volume building business became an annual 30- to 40-project volume industry within a brief period. The interest earned from these small loans coupled with the principal payment provided a regular good source of revenue for many years to come.

With the company owning the majority of the shares in the Henry County venture, an effort was made to sell these shares. They represented partial ownership in 40-plus acres of reasonably valuable property. A prominent developer and builder named Gerald Hudgins, whose office was in the area where the property was located, was contacted. Conversation revealed that this young man was much like the other people alluded to in the previous paragraph. He, too, was a little short on cash! By this time I was a near genius at putting this type puzzle together. Provident possessed the *anything*; Mr. Hudgins became the *anybody*; and since there was no money owed on the asset, the arrangements were easy to make.

In shorter time than a small playful kitten could get untangled from a roll of knitting yarn, a deal was put together. The customer would be required to make interest-only annual payments until the property was developed, and the principal was to be paid as the buildings were completed and the land released. Within the time frame of a few short months, all the property was developed, and the company was paid in full. This effort began to pour some extra funds into the company coffers, and each month it became stronger. The whole debacle was much like brer rabbit fighting the tar baby. The fact that the company was stuck fast was an indisputable fact. However, as brer fox had built a big fire with which to destroy our company, the heat of the fire had only served as an agent to free us! Now, at least one paw was unstuck, and it was just a matter of enduring the heat until all paws and the bumped head were released!

Another brush with disaster

If this treatise included every encounter this company had with the apple cart being upset, it would sound like a broken record. Unfortunately, Mr. Roget did not supply enough synonyms for disaster; therefore, possibly before I am finished, you will read the same flag statement!

One of the company's greatest assets was a 50+ acre tract of land located in Gwinnett County, fronting on Tribble Mill Road. This property was situated several miles away from the county seat, Lawrenceville, and was obviously years away from profitable development. The new president, not totally aware as to the physical location of this property, made a trip to Lawrenceville to search county records for the location and also for any encumbrances against the property. The findings were alarming. Property taxes had not been paid in a number of years. Several hundred dollars in back taxes were due coupled with penalties and interest. The tax commissioner was in the process of foreclosing on the property for the payment of taxes. This was just another of the comedies of mistakes made by people who knew better and without excuse. Howbeit the taxes had to be paid, and fortunately there were adequate funds in the treasury to pay these levies.

In an effort to convert this asset to a revenue producing unit, the developer who had purchased the Henry County property was contacted. This elbow grease really paid off. An agreement was entered with Mr. Hudgins to purchase this property with a custom designed financing plan. This accord embraced a down payment of $15,000 plus, with interest payment only for the first five years; and the next five years, principal and interest payments were designed to pay the remaining balance. The company financed $135,000 in this deal at 10 percent simple interest.

The plan was a dream come true and placed the company in a position to receive an additional income of several thousand dollars annually over the next decade. These funds were going to fit beautifully into the company plans to re-enter the church financing market. The tar baby continued to melt, and slowly all the members of the company body were being freed. The arm of church funding was now free, and it was to gain in strength each month as the company began to RISE AGAIN!

Let's take a short break before your eyes cross from reading this lengthy chapter, and I'll try to re-establish some family communications which have suffered greatly since I have begun the task of reporting the history of this company. Hurry back, for the report is going to get better!

Chapter Seven
The Music Begins

T here is no music to the ear of the builder which will equal the sweet notes created by buzzing saws and pounding hammers. The multiple sounds created by many workers around a sizeable construction project provides as much harmony to my ears as a 50-piece symphony orchestra. I had been so busy for several months putting out fires until there was no time left for constructive purposes other than the deep satisfaction of knowing that we were winning the battle of survival. The time would come shortly when this company we had worked so hard to save would actually be in shape financially to assist in a sizeable church construction project.

The city of Lilburn, Georgia, was chosen as the place to strike up the band! The company's vice president Jon Ostrom lived here. He was well-known and established in the area, and the net worth of his financial statement caused the eyes of bankers to bulge like a bullfrog's eyes. When we went to the bank to do business, the bankers met us at the door and were ready to extend liberal credit to the company as long as Jon and I would sign the personal guarantee. I occasionally told Jon that I felt like Jethro walking around with Jed Clampett.

This company owes a tremendous debt of gratitude to the Ostrom family for extending their arm of friendship and unselfish help during those months of extreme crisis. I remember a friendly gathering in the law offices of

Charles J. Alford, Jr. for a noon meal engagement, when he told Jon and me that he saw no way for the company to survive. Also, he thought our efforts were unwise and in vain. He knew that the company would be required to operate on the "coattail" of responsible people who would be required to extend their financial necks to obtain credit for basic operations. The mammoth task of restoring the lending arm, as we were to learn, was going to require the joint efforts of both of us. Essentially, what was going to be required was for us to pledge every personal asset we owned in order to secure funds for church lending purposes.

The area of personal liability was of utmost concern to the attorney. He and Jon had built a solid client-friend relationship over a period of years, and I feel sure that he was afraid that either of us might jeopardize our financial status. However, every time I would even entertain a thought about recanting, the wonderful Holy Spirit would help me remember some of the dear old saints of God who had invested the last dime of their savings into a company that they thought would exhibit the highest standards of Christian conduct. This confidence had been betrayed. There was but one creditable option, we felt; and that was to go forward, sink or swim!

Personally, I did not have a problem with the risk, for I knew the cause was just and right! If risk were the only factor, the task would have been a piece of cake. But we were to learn that RISK has a multitude of disciples. I don't think there was a single member of the risk family that we didn't come to know on a first-name basis! The board of directors knew that if this deeply troubled company didn't make it, we would bear the entire blame for its default. As far as I was concerned, there were no options. At that time I was 56 years of age, and I had not been associated with a single failing business effort in my lifetime; and by the help and grace of God, I didn't intend for the dead albatross of Provident Investment Corporation to establish a failing precedence in my retirement years.

The scheme of loan participation

The amount of money the Faith Outreach Church building project was going to require was in the vicinity of $150,000. There were some very positive positions in the projected building effort. The church owned several acres of very valuable land just off the Stone Mountain Freeway in the city of Lilburn. This property was debt-free, and the church had several thousand dollars in a building account. However, with all of these pluses, there was a deficit of more than $80,000 that would be required to make the project work. These funds would have to come from the bank with personal guarantees by Ostrom and Summerlin.

A date and time were set to launch the attack at the bank. Jon called his banker and confirmed a time for the appointment. A list of documents to be provided at the meeting was given including a personal financial statement which provided a place to list every marketable asset each of us owned. Now if you don't think that last requirement doesn't require some soul searching, you may want to try it sometime. Laying your life savings on the line to guarantee a loan for a church. In my case more than 35 years of labor and in Jon's case a corresponding period. Let me tell you that if you don't live in the spirit and believe in your cause, you had better stay on the porch and not attempt to run with the big dogs!

The Ostrom family believed in the cause they were pursuing, and that was good enough for me. They were manifesting more than a sailor's courage to team with a company that was standing on trembling earth, but collectively there was no doubt that we would make the project work. We desperately needed the addition of a solid church loan in the company's loan portfolio, so we fired both barrels, and at least made a lot of noise. I grimaced when I remembered an auto tag I had bought at a gag shop sometime earlier which said, "We are spending our children's inheritance." I had no idea that the fun could vanish so quickly. I doubtless would have severely criticized any one of our children if they had dared to engage in a scheme that appeared as unwise as the one their father was entering into. Like I said a little earlier in this chapter, if you are going to live on the edge like Jon and I were about to begin, you had better be standing on some solid ground and have an open channel to the glory world.

The meeting at the bank was very pleasant and rewarding. The requested loan amount would be made available, and there would not be any collateral required but the personal endorsement of the president and vice president. I noticed a grin on the banker's face similar to the one I heard about when the cheshire cat ate the canary which belonged to his owner..."What bird?" He sheepishly smiled as he tucked the financial statements of his two new customers into the files of his banking institution. I feel sure he slept well that night for there was doubtless not a loan in the bank's portfolio that was as well-secured as the one he had just closed!

A plan comes together

I'm sure that each trade in life has a downside as well as the mountaintop glory. The building business is no different from others in many ways. But the time when a building begins to come to life is a thing of intrinsic beauty. After months of planning, changing, redrawing and running an obstacle course equal to "The Battle of Bull Run," the builder and the owner share a pride of satisfaction that is not surpassed by any trade kinsman.

The church (Faith Outreach) had spent months in rented buildings, none of which was to be their permanent home. The time had finally come; the apprenticeship was over. The sound of heavy equipment, the buzzing of power saws, the crisp cracks from busy hammers were full testimony that a fulfilled dream was in the making. The full-size basement floor rose out of the ground board by board like a giant to proclaim its steadfastness. The second floor that followed began to cover the landscape, bringing a beauty that added grace to the sloping hillsides. Each day passing was much like adding another page to a book by a passionate author. A few more chapters to write and the book of building Faith Outreach church would be complete. The time was soon to come when the greater part of the worship house would arrive. I recently read the account of I Kings, chapters eight and nine, where the sacred pages unfold the culminating acts of the temple construction.

The spirit of the grand architect was satisfied. The builders' tools were silenced after months of labor. The final trees had fallen in the forest. The stone quarry had yielded the final stone which was shaped by the master masons and fitted into the grand walls making all of the walls a single piece. The artificiers had tooled the last meaningful symbol on the wings of the cheribums and seraphims.

The temple bore complete witness to the skill and dedication of a myriad of skilled craftsmen and laborers. However, the building was not yet complete. The tenant must arrive before the grand finale! The illustrious works of Solomon faded like a phantom in the night as the glory of the Lord filled the temple. Faith Outreach Church was soon to begin its real God-ordained ministry, the sacred trust of leading souls to Christ. There were many to come from all walks of life, but those who were there and experienced the birth and life of a church building structure, would harbor a near sacred treasure. The blessing that comes with the fortune of having lived in a certain day ordained by the great Creator carries a reward to treasure in the years to come.

As the day of dedication drew near, a busy laity scurried about in search of a multitude of essentials to make the Lord's house complete. Much like a hive of busy bees, they sped in every direction, gathering the precious nectar from every plant and tree, whose timely process had supplied a generous offering to all who were willing to make the sacrifice of labor to dip from the fragrant blossoms. This abundant spread was a provision made possible by

Faith Outreach, Stone Mountain, Georgia

the hand of a kind heavenly Father. Offerings were placed in every nook and cranny of the worship facility. Each gift was placed much like the arrangement of the notes by a famous composer on sheets of music, designed to call the combined attention of a vast symphony orchestra to a single note of harmony. The single focus was designed to bless the hearts of mankind when they dared to gather within the sacred nave and halls of the sanctuary.

There was not a single faction of all the vast work force who was as proud of the complete worship facility as the board of directors of Provident Investment Corporation. We were witnessing a miracle in the making. The frail body of a severely wounded company had taken a giant step in the direction of recovery. It could be done. There would of necessity be required an extended time for complete recovery, but the real crisis was over. The company had deposited in the trust of a responsible congregation all of its funds together with the moneys borrowed from the coffers of a regulated lending institution. The bank was expecting the return of their loan plus a handsome user's fee in the form of interest. No one seemed to exhibit an ounce of doubt that the agreement would be honored. The trust was a mutual concern, and each party had great confidence that each would perform to the highest degree in this very noble undertaking.

The posts, with a speed greater than the ancient pony express, carried the message of the great dedication day to a number of cities and communities throughout the state of Georgia. The invitation was as broad as the one issued by Jesus and reported by the venerable gospel writer:

"Whosoever will, let him come." The gracious proffer seemed to have the compelling effect of a court summons. As the announced hour arrived, invited guests, together with dedicated parishioners, assembled in the lovely building to witness the public offering of a pledge to give and dedicate the building and grounds to almighty God, through Jesus Christ the Lord. The purpose was for the spreading of the Gospel to the ends of the earth.

The members of the board of directors and their wives assembled as a family to blend into the harmonious affair. I had witnessed and participated in building dedicatorial services on a much larger scale, including one church my construction company built which seated more than 5,000 people. However, the dedication of the church in Lilburn carried a special dimension all its own. The spirited music and singing visibly expressed the pride and satisfaction of all participants.

The closing of the great service had a tremendous bonding effect upon the congregation, yet one could detect that it also marked a parting of ways. The enthusiastic membership and friends would follow a path clearly delineated by the Holy Spirit to spread the "good news" to all who would hear. The path as clearly visible to the leadership of Provident Investment Corporation led in another direction where the search for funds and a site upon which to invest them was to be sought. The harder part of this great enigma would be acquiring moneys from a reluctant society which was totally aware of the past history of a company that did not seem to attract their trust.

The successful completion of the church building in

Lilburn demonstrated clearly the ability and skills of the company's management team. It also confirmed an earlier conviction of the wisdom of the company in pursuing churches requiring small loans not to exceed $60,000. The reasoning was multifarious. First, we could reach more areas of the state, and each project was to be a real confidence booster. The hostile spirit of a betrayed stockholder body would diminish as the company moved forward very slowly but in a manner as discreet as Smith and Barney. We would imitate the pattern established by a great American investment institution, "We would make money the old fashioned way; WE WOULD EARN IT!" The task would not be easy, but none of the things the management team had encountered thus far had been easy! The journey had been much like one of the wise old southern proverbs:"It was like the cat eating the grubbing hoe – rough and slow!"

Recounting the rewards

The completion of the church at Lilburn provided an opportunity to assess the full impact that this loan, and others to be made in the future, would have on the coffers and accounting reports of our company. A decision made by the board earlier, to charge comparable loan origination fees and interest rates imposed by other regulated lending institutions in the same area, proved to be wise and was also accepted very favorably by the church obtaining the loan. Most of the banks and federal savings and loan associations were charging fees which translated into earnings amounting to 3 to 3 1/2 percent. This percentage figure was exacted on the entire loan. The church or individual making the loan had the option of paying these fees in cash at the loan closing or having them added to the loan package. The net effect was the same for the company; these fees were direct earnings and would be reflected in the income section of the accounting reports for the year they were collected.

The loan for the Faith Outreach Church was near the $150,000 range. Therefore, an amount of $5,000 plus was added immediately to the net earnings figure. The transaction was merely a penciled entry on paper, but it represented earnings which were placed in the loans section of the accounting records, and these fees began immediately to earn interest for the company at the same rate as the loan. It becomes really easy for anyone to see what the earnings potential of the company could be if the funds could be secured to make the loans to a number of congregations which were anxiously waiting. The rewards to be earned were ample if ways and means could be found to obtain the much-needed funds to set the loan machine in operation on a perpetual basis. This was the stated objective of a dedicated board of directors and staff. The resolve and desire to see this ambition accomplished permeated the fiber and being of the entire staff. It was not a matter of *if* this were possible, but rather *when*. The time element depended entirely on how well we could convince those who had the funds to release them for such a noble cause as providing money to a congregation to assist them in building a worship facility for the purpose of propagating the gospel of Jesus Christ. It did not matter what name they chose to put over the door or on the signpost out in front of the church. The attitude of the company was if the body were promoting the cause of spreading the gospel, we wanted to be a part of that effort and stood ready to join the hands and ranks of those who were dedicated to this cause.

A mixture of loans

The addition of good sound church loans to the company's portfolio was obviously the soundest and most prudent course to pursue. Albeit, there was a downside to this course, for the banking institutions from which the company was going to be required to borrow a portion of the funds needed to fund these projects, looked with near disdain upon church loans. As I have stated in the genesis chapter of this treatise, church collateral is not the type of security a banker is comfortable with and especially if the loan is geared to a congregation in another city and county. There was also the element of public scrutiny coupled with the possibility that at a future date the company's stock could be publicly offered. These and other viable considerations caused the board to examine the possibility of a loan mixture of first mortgage home loans together with the church loans.

The first approach toward accomplishing this measure was to take advantage of another existing treasure which could be capitalized on, financing – the pastorium or a residence sought by the church pastor which were already securely placed in the private sector financing. These loans were to be had for the asking. The church pastors of America are one of the most respected professions and credit-worthy groups to be found. Therefore, the company made a decision to test the waters in this vital area. The search results were simply wonderful. The fees to be earned were equated to the church loan formula, similar to the church loan, and found to be most desirable to add to the loan portfolio. These loans were actually more profitable than the church loans. Some of the underlying reasons were: The loans were smaller and the turnover time shorter. At the time of this writing, we have approximately 15 percent home loans and are well on the way to accomplishing the established objective.

There remains a vast enigma about how apparently wise and well qualified banking officials view church loans as opposed to first mortgage home loans. They will go to almost any extreme to make a credit-worthy pastor a loan to buy himself a house, and yet when the same pastor inquires about a loan for the church he pastors, a cold shoulder is turned by the same officer who exhibited great warmth when a home loan was requested! After many years of experience of working with the greatest people on earth and extending loans amounting strongly in the seven figure columns, I remained mystified as to why banks and lending institutions do not actively solicit good church loans. Although I still don't know how a red cow can eat green grass and drink branch water and give white milk and yellow butter, but I surely do like to drink the milk and eat the butter. Until I learn better and get it all figured out, I am going to make as many good church and parsonage loans as there are funds available to make them with. They are indeed the best loans available in America today!

Chapter Eight

Adding Speed to the Earnings Process

I have shared the conviction for years that one of the great failures of mankind is the inability to see what talents or assets one possesses and the potential of these gifts when properly applied. This problem has apparently existed since mankind was created. The book of Exodus reports the deficiency Moses possessed in the early part of chapter four. Moses had carried the shepherd's rod for an extended period. All the rod had ever been to Moses was a shepherd's rod. However, the Lord caused him to see that this familiar hand tool could be a great deal more than he had been using it for. God taught Moses that if he would enroll his rod in His obedience school that it would serve multiple purposes. God's first lesson of instruction was for him to "cast it on the ground." There remains a great enigma about this encounter between Moses and the Lord, but one of the things I have learned is that everything has a diversity of purpose when being used obediently. Possessing this bit of biblical knowledge has caused me to search continuously for every possible use of anything at my disposal.

The company was making excellent progress by every creditable standard. However, it was so far in the hole that it would take years for it to fully recover unless there could be a bonanza discovered somewhere in the company's arsenal inventory. I have spent a great part of my adult life in travel and learned that this transit time could be very productive if I thought and planned during these periods of quiet time. I spent my early years from 18 years of age to 25 in the military service of the U.S. Air Force. I have flown over vast areas of this good earth, and many of these flights were lengthy. There was ample time for thinking and reading, and I partook from both very generously.

Applying these habits has served me in good stead. I have always believed that with God's help you can think your way out of any situation, regardless of how difficult it may seem.

I spent countless hours in travel in privately owned vehicles. While on one of these thought trips one day in my car, the idea occurred to me that since the building projects the company was involved with required so much of my time, why did not the company charge for this knowledge? I had acquired extensive experience from the building business to which I have alluded in previous chapters. My experience as a builder had covered a 28-plus year span. We had built everything from a small three-bedroom house to large commercial store buildings, banks, and churches. These churches had seating capacities from 150 to one that seated more than 5,000! I felt on this particular day the Lord was saying to me, "What is that in thine hand? You could use the rod (talent) for Kingdom purposes!"

The Good Lord helped me to see that it was indeed

laudable to offer these talents for His service. To exact a fee for their use was neither wrong nor inappropriate. However, if I were to use them in this manner, I would remain dedicated to a principle I have followed all my life. These charges would be fair, and they would be extended on a no-charge basis if a small church were in need of such to help them obtain a building to worship in. My 40 years' experience as a home missions pastor had taught me the value and importance of a helping hand while laboring in this urgent harvest field. There were many times when these building efforts would have suffered had it not been for the cost-free skillful and able hands which were extended while these churches were in the building stages.

Perhaps a bit of information about some of the these experiences will be helpful for the reader to better understand why I have developed a near sacred approach toward helping struggling churches. As a home missions pastor/worker, I supported my family through full-time secular employment. My skills and formal training had been in the administrative and personnel management field. I knew nothing about the engineering, mechanical, and construction phases of the building business. Necessity dictated that I depend upon others to supply the needed skills. Neither time nor space will permit me to share the vast gifts of labor which were timely provided to get these buildings completed for orderly worship. Suffice it to say that this help came when needed. On one occasion, the county warden permitted county prisoners to lay the concrete blocks for the first building attempt. This

Blue Ridge Mountain Assembly of God Church
Cleveland, Georgia

Clayton First Assembly of God, Clayton, Georgia

Church of Christ Written in Heaven, Macon, Georgia

Word of Truth, Macon, Georgia
Old Building (above) and new building (below)

True Light Tabernacle, Cartersville, Georgia.
Old building (above), new building (below).

First Assembly of God, Fitzgerald (top)
Greater Zion Hill Baptist, Macon (bottom)

building still stands today in a small community in South Georgia after more than 40 years of continuous use. The fact is that the total debt which existed at the time of completion was less than $300 for more than 1,200 square feet of church building. This testimony readily reveals the amount of help that church received through helping hands!

Setting the machine in operation

The city of Valdosta, Georgia, was chosen as the site to launch the joint effort of building and financing a church building project. Here again mother necessity played her hand. (The company a few years before had financed a small mission work for the Evangel Temple Church, a small minority group led by Reverend Henry Wright II.) Their record of performance under Pastor Wright had been nearly spectacular. In a few short years, they had outgrown the building and were in desperate need of a new facility. They already owned ample land upon which to build. However, the congregation was not able to afford the luxury of hiring a contractor to build the facility. The "turn key" approach was simply not affordable.

The church had settled on a plan which was used in Panama City, Florida, by the author while building the last missions church he began. This approach saved the church several thousand dollars in plans cost. This choice plus the decisive advantage of having built the church before was extremely advantageous. Five years before, the building was completed at a cost of approximately $460,000. The building would comfortably seat approximately 360 people and appeared to be exactly what Pastor

Wright and his congregation needed. The only problem at this juncture was that Evangel Temple's congregation could not afford the payments on a $460,000 mortgage. Bids taken from competent building contractors in the Lowndes County area indicated that the building would cost in the vicinity of $600,000. This startling revelation told all of us that "this dog won't hunt!" The church could not afford a monthly mortgage payment much over $3,000. This figure was exactly one half of the projected monthly cost; so it was back to the drawing board!

Meaningful downsizing

The new church was to be located adjacent to the old building, making it available for classrooms and other social functions. The great wisdom of Dr. Henry Wright II.to downsize, dropping the classrooms and social hall from the proposed plan, would hopefully enable him to get a sanctuary which would accommodate more than 400 people. A new series of cost estimates were completed, and it appeared that a zero profit approach could help us to get the church finished for around $300,000. There was no one in Lowndes County who agreed with us, but we were confident that if we wisely used "What we had in our hands" that the Lord would provide the difference. Lending officials from other reputable banking institutions have great difficulty in attaching a meaningful value to "what the Lord provides."

In the absence of this great financial wisdom, a decision was made to proceed with the building project on a cost plus 10 percent basis. I will always be appreciative of the giant faith exhibited by one of the greatest congregations in America, the Evangel Temple family! This is a church that has a daily prayer meeting from noon until one o'clock. Many of the members and friends forfeit their lunch hour and come to the church for prayer during this established time. This prayer meeting has been going on for more than 25 years at the time of this writing, and I am told that it is greater now than ever. I have known the value and importance of prayer all of my Christian life which spans a time of more than 45 years. I have witnessed the impossible become a workable solution time and again through prayer. Therefore, I was totally unafraid to join hands with Pastor Wright to witness a miracle in the making!

Construction begins

Provident people (now you need to understand that there were two people working for Provident and the secretary was in the office) provided all the engineering work for this project. Much of this engineering working was subterranean excavation. The foregoing sentence is a lot of fancy words, when simply put, means "ditch digging." This is the type of work of little glory and self exalting praise; however, it is the most important phase of a building project. This excavation work was accomplished almost totally by "Provident people" aided by a small John Deere backhoe which was loaned by a friend for a small user's fee. The foundation work which usually comprises approximately 10 percent of the total cost was completed for several hundred dollars less than the anticipated figure. Therefore, the project was well under way, and the projected goal for this work was significantly under the budget. So, we were off with flying colors!

Friendships pay big dividends

My experience as a home missions worker/pastor had enabled me to become well acquainted with every industry and supplier of the church building trade. Over the years, we had established highly creditable relationships with these people, and they extended every courtesy and cost concession possible to any church building project we were associated with. Some of the most helpful folks in America are from the firm of Structural Wood Systems. Mr. Carlton Whittle heads this great firm together with his office staff and factory in Greenville, Alabama. These good folk provided all the engineering work, shop drawings, and manufacturing of the laminated wood works and other components for the type buildings that we primarily use in building and/or finance.

The relationship with these people began in 1977 when a need surfaced for a very complex wood structural system for a sizeable church project. The octagonal-shaped sanctuary would seat approximately 5,000 people. This building was built under contract for the Independent Holiness Church in Albany, Georgia, by a firm owned by the writer known as Summerlin Construction Company. The size and complexity of the project necessitated several trips to the home office of the Structural Wood System firm. During the time of the engineering and designing of the church inner structure, a good solid friendship began to form that since has developed into a strong ongoing working relationship.

From the stance of this lengthy relationship, a trip was

made to Greenville, Alabama, to renew acquaintances and place an order for the laminated wood structural system for the Evangel Temple Church. The highly creditable experiences of the past 10 years eliminated the need for extensive credit checks and other delays which are customary for newcomers to the specialty building field. All the work projects undertaken by Structural Wood System come under the hood of originality, and components they manufacture must be used in the building for which they are designed. A dead albatross hung around your neck would be a piece of cake compared to a specially designed building which would not fit into a proposed foundation design. Albeit, these good people never question our requests and have always provided quality manufactured components for our building requests.

The Evangel Temple project was no different. The request was cheerfully processed and bore a design as original as a walker hound dog! In my opinion, churches are much like people. Each has its own special design, to be fitted on a special landscape which tends to enhance its originality. The Evangel Church building is located a short distance from Moody Air Force base. The aero designed front of the lovely sanctuary bears a similar design to the highly sophisticated F-16 fighter planes which are stationed nearby and frequently fly over the hallowed grounds of Evangel Temple Church.

By the time the ground work was completed and the finished concrete floors were in place, a huge truck arrived, bearing the beautiful beams, arches and purlins, wrapped in colorful well bound coverings which would have graced an Egyptian mummy! Waiting all-terrain lifts and cranes, engaged by prior arrangement, began the delicate task of unloading and placing each group of these components on a temporary storage site. As soon as the unloading chore was completed and truck released, the giant crane, under the astute control of a highly skilled operator, was forced to extend its neck like a lazy turtle to a nearly frightening height. In a matter of a few minutes the crane operator swung the incredible neck over to the stack of half arches and slowly lowered the cable fed big round headache ball to a man's height. A rigging apparatus was proportionately spaced by a small ground crew to ensure swift aerial transit to the huge awaiting iron shoe on the solid floor foundation. The incredible neck began to rewind the long cable tongue and simultaneously swing the completed arch to the base shoes. Stopped high above in a precise spot, the headache ball descended slowly with the arch gracefully swinging in the crisp spring breeze. The bases of the heavy arches were swung into place with the aid of long tow lines in the simple hands of two laborers. The fit was as snug as a surgeon's glove. Every step to follow this initial placement would serve as a strengthening device to weld the strong fabricated timbers into a single giant structure! As I have observed numerous buildings come together, I have always hoped that the congregations who were to occupy these edifices would be as strong and as closely knit together as the building they were to worship in.

Many hands make the job easier

I have always enjoyed the biblical account of the manpower scheme designed by the wisdom of Solomon. The Jewish work force to labor with the Sidonians was a hefty crew of 30,000 men with 3,300 supervisors. The plan divided the labor force in three equal increments and allowed each segment to work 30 days in Lebanon and return home for a 60-day leave. You know, that was not a bad deal at all! They worked four months out of each 12 and enjoyed an eight-month vacation! I have always supposed that all of us are working too much, and I could be a strong advocate of this biblical plan! Although the Provident crew could not afford the luxury of imitating this luscious biblical example, we did enjoy the luxury of going home every night.

Even though an extremely sparse work force was used while building Evangel Temple, we did enjoy the presence of a complete staff of sub-contractors, who had been working together for years as members of the Summerlin Construction team. This able body of dedicated craftsmen systematically attacked the building project, each bringing special expertise to effect strength, comfort and convenience to a building that would house one of America's finest Christian congregations, the flock of Dr. Henry Wright II!

A time frame of six months had been established initially for the construction of the swept-wing designed worship facility. This time element appeared to be adequate, especially if mother nature cooperated with the graces of good weather and timely arrival of the needed building components. All these were enjoyed, as a sizeable total work force forged a landmark in an area of Lowndes which

**Original church building, Evangel Temple Church
Valdosta, Georgia**

Front view of Evangel Temple and side view of old church.

**Front view, Evangel Temple Church
Valdosta, Georgia**

would dominate the landscape for many years to come. The entire project enjoyed one of the most harmonious working relationships which has ever been undertaken. To my knowledge, there was not one discordant note in the entire symphony. All the ingredients were present almost every day to ignite an explosion: limited funds, hot sultry summer weather, and many other elements numerous enough to fill a powder keg. However, everyone refused to give one foot of ground to the church's enemy, Satan, and the building was headed for the final stretch with sufficient momentum to finish the race.

Recounting the cost

Long before the able writing and sound counsel offered by outstanding authors like Norman-Vincent Peale, Dale Carnegie, Stephen Covey and others, a dear old friend and neighbor imparted some sound advice to me as solid as either of these collegial orators. He had never heard of the power of positive thinking or the win-win, win-lose proposition. However, he gave me a measure of advice that became a way of life with me and has served me for a span well beyond the 50-year mark. His philosophy was: "No deal is a good deal unless it is a good deal for both parties." He practiced this sound Christian principle until the day of his death many years ago. I have, doubtless very feebly, tried to imitate his great example.

This first adventure of erecting a church with a manifold goal of minimum cost and a very rigid final loan figure was an absolute must for the Evangel Temple congregation and Provident Investment Corporation. Of necessity, it had to be a good deal for both parties. When the final figures were catalogued and the time of reckoning arrived, every-one was very pleasantly surprised to learn that the build-ing was ready for dedication, and we were within budget! I continue to thank the Lord until this day for this mira-cle. The total loan figure was approximately $316,000, and this figure included the remaining indebtedness on the old church mortgage. The building included a balcony which seats approximately 100 people and upstairs offices for pastor and two assistant pastors. The final cost of a little more than $30 per square foot was not equal to the cost of erecting a one-story residential dwelling in the year 1987. This type of results defy logical explanation, and those who do not believe in miracles will still be trying to figure this one out when the Lord returns for His church!

The sixty-four thousand dollar question

How did Provident fare? When the project began, Pastor Wright and his staff agreed that each week we would pay the bills, and each account would receive the 10 percent cost plus surcharge. This amount was charged against the loan account each week, and when the build-ing was finished and the last check was written, all the bills were paid in full, including almost $30,000 for the cof-fers of a very needy company. Even though the cash regis-ter did not ring up a $30,000 cash sale, the equity of the stockholding body was increased by this amount plus all other funds gained through interest earned!

This rewarding effort did miracles for the morale of a stockholder body. Until this time, they had every reason for nothing but gloom and dismay! Now, we could look in the face of a jubilant congregation and shocked group of stock owners and say to them both, "We have made money the old-fashioned way; we have earned it." We had been able to work a deal which had been a good deal for both parties. As far as I know, which has the vantage point of almost 10 years, Pastor Henry Wright II continues to think he got a good deal. As a personal reward, I received the extra bonus of a pinched nerve in my neck, resulting from having looked up so much. An injury sustained years before had been aggravated. I guess I'm probably the only man in the world who gets tortured for looking up. But I understand that is the direction the church is going, and I plan to keep my sights in the upward direction!

A dedication day not soon to be forgotten

The Evangel Temple Church family was prepared to move into their new worship facility in the precise time frame. The building was finished to the high architectural and engineering standards under the skilled and critical eye of Jack Holland, P.E. He has more than a half century of sound experience and training and has been associated with some of the most distinctive building projects in the Southeast. He gave very generously of his time and services to ensure that the Evangel Temple structure was built to the highest possible standards. Requiring special mouldings and decorative trim work is a trait he is especially noted for.

The author owned the finest mouldings and millworks shop in the southeastern United States. This shop was manned by some of the finest craftsmen in America. Wood mouldings and many different styles of wood trim were designed and created in the shop located in Moultrie,

Georgia. Many of the outstanding churches and homes throughout the southeastern United States have been adorned with the wood trims and cabinetry work that was manufactured by A & S Millworks. No horses were spared when the time came for the supply of trim work. The shop had gone into a semi-retired state in 1981, but when the need for specialty material arose, the old crew swung back into operation. Two men with nearly 100 years of woodworking experience manned the complex machines and created the special woodwork to fill the critical dimensions specified for Evangel Temple. Mr. J. C. Goodroe, who came to work for A & S Millworks when he was 15 years old, has never had another job. He remains in the employment of the A & S firm as of the time of this writing. Mr. Leroy Moore, a native of the state of West Virginia, was discharged from the U.S. Air Force at the close of World War II at Spence Field in Moultrie. He married Judge Bryant's daughter and came to work for the millwork shop in the spring of 1946. He was doubtless one of America's finest millwrights. These two outstanding men used their many years of skill and experience to produce the best possible decorative trim for a very deserving building.

The finished trim work was cut and fitted by the distinguished crew from the A & S Millwork shop. The type of work which was performed by these men would have graced the superb work accomplished by the illustrious crew who worked on Solomon's Temple! Someone surmised that the finish work on Evangel Temple was much like a jeweler making a golden ring. The work of forming and making the perfect circle is just a prelude to the real work of splendor. The real test is when the precious stone is placed in the golden bracket! From the moment the stone is placed, all eyes henceforth are focused on the sparkling beauty of the glittering gem!

Distant visitors share dedicatorial festivities

No one would ever guess that Dr. Henry Wright II is from the empire state. He was born and spent most of his childhood years in the Big Apple! The curt, well-spoken English, which is usually distinctively characteristic of most northern folk, doubtless was a trait of the huge framed, kind-hearted and generous Henry Wright. However, the northern dialect has long been replaced by a slow southern speech that would grace any southern plantation!

Obviously, the only thing Pastor Wright lost from his northern connection was his mannerism of speech. His firm connection with a host of friends from his home state has never diminished. This was evident by the arrival of two chartered Greyhound buses loaded with a small army of friends who had received the good news about the new church building and the splendid Christian work which had been performed by one of New York state's favorite sons. Each friend had arranged to have an extended weekend off from work and had provided the funds necessary to defray the travel expenses to south Georgia. In all more than 80 people, family and friends, had made the arduous journey. None of them had lost any of their joy or enthusiasm. They arrived singing the hosannas and praises to the Great God Almighty!

The guest speaker, a very successful pastor from New York state, was also a very dear friend of Pastor Wright.

He had traveled the many miles also to share in the special accomplishment of a person whom he had discipled and influenced to enter the work of the Lord. His power-packed message gave full attest to his godly pride in a young man who was being recognized as an outstanding pastor and leader of the flock of God.

A testimony that dwarfed the dedication service

As the register of special guests was being served and each guest asked to give a very brief speech, the printed program did not include the name of the grand old saint and godmother of Henry Wright II. However, she was courteously asked to give a brief testimony. She began by telling how she would walk down the streets in New York City toward the church gathering up children from all walks of life to lead them to the church she attended. Here they would be able to become acquainted with the Lord Jesus Christ. She related how each block would yield a child or two as she continued traveling in the direction of the church.

Children are naturally attracted by other children, and as Mother Murden related in her testimony, the crowd began to grow as she walked along the streets humming the old songs of Zion. She shared the heart-warming experience about when she came by the house where little Henry Wright II lived. She wiped the tears from her eyes as she told about pausing in the street long enough to ask the child if he would like to go to the house of the Lord. He responded with a resounding yes! He was told to be ready the next time she came by, and he would surely be welcome to join the small youth army and join in the church worship services.

That child she invited to become a member of the greatest army in the world is still in service for his Commander-in-Chief. He presently sat on the platform among a host of special invited guests with tears streaming down his cheeks. He doubtless was wondering, as were a number of us, would he be sitting here on this special day, if a dear old saint of God had not cared enough about children to take the time to spread some of God's kindness along the way! She stopped occasionally to catch the tears as she shared a testimony that would make it difficult for any minister to step forward and further arouse the worship passions of a congregation that was presently mystified by the enigma WHAT IF? !

She closed her testimony and asked for permission to lead the congregation in a grand old chorus. The approving eyes of a tear-dimmed church family followed as Mother Murden led the familiar spiritual, "I Am Blessed." She moved out into the aisles of the church and led that chorus with five hundred voices including my wife and me. An order of apology is certainly in order to the great speaker who followed Mother Murden's chorus leading; but I honestly don't remember one word of his message. I do recall that it was eloquently presented under the fire and anointing of the Holy Spirit. I am sure that many of us who have been fortunate enough to be called to the discipleship of Christ have witnessed dozens of times when some dear old saint under the profound leadership of the Holy Spirit has "stolen our thunder" from our message by obedience to the Spirit!

Chapter Nine

Smooth Sailing

Shallow waters are the avowed enemies of sailing. No captain nor crew dare relax as long as their ship has the threat of treacherous waters. It is only after the passing through these waters of peril that the crew can relax and concentrate its efforts on sound navigation and reaching established goals. There are many ports of call that the "Miss Provident" will make enroute to a final destination which hopefully will not be reached until God's plan for His church is culminated. Our motto is the same as the divine mandate: we will "Occupy until He comes."

No need for a sales force

Most companies the size of Provident spend a large percentage of their budget annually on a sizeable sales force or massive advertising efforts to attract customers. Salesmen are constantly seeking ways and means to locate prospects which they hope to convert into the customer circle. I worked a number of years as an accounting supervisor for Swift and Company, the largest meat processors in America. During these years I watched the frantic pace of a sales force that beat on every store and market door in the area in search of business. After long hours, week after week, there were extra sales meetings and blitzes they were required to attend. Why? In search of business!

With no intention of being flippant, I must truthfully

report that during the 20 years that I have served this company, I have not stepped off the porch in search of a worthy customer with which to entrust our funds! I don't know of another company that can support so great a claim!

A trip to the bank

Again I suppose another story of a personal incident which happened years ago will add some insight into the conundrum. In the mid 1950's on a Saturday morning, I went down to the local bank to attempt to entice the good banker to make me a personal loan to assist in the purchase of a much-needed automobile. Upon arriving at the bank and noting the room filled with folks waiting to see him, the thought occurred to me that everybody's car must have worn out at the same time, and they need the banker's assistance.

I took my place in the quiet room where there was a silence that surpassed a mortuary viewing room. I was measurably impressed with the varied expressions on the faces of the people, as their anxiety surfaced while waiting their turn to see the banker. I was in my mid-20's at the time and had little experience in dealing with bankers about obtaining the use of their money and especially for such a non-essential use as buying a car. As I quickly looked over the crowd to catch another glance of their faces, I wondered which face should I imitate that would enhance my chances of obtaining the loan.

There was a very pleasant looking gentleman in the waiting group who returned a winning smile each time he had eye contact with anyone else in the room. So I began to imitate his pleasantness by casting my best smile to those who were frequently catching a glimpse of my mug and doubtless speculating about what such a young and obviously inexperienced person was doing in the bank loan room. Have you ever wondered about the thoughts other folks have of you, especially when there is ample time to do nothing but sit and pretend to peruse a long-expired magazine? Most folks will hastily dispose of dated magazines and other publications, but in waiting rooms people grab them like they are hot off the press! I'll bet they use them like I did as a farce to look at and study the faces of others.

One of the greatest lessons I ever learned

One of the many thoughts which raced through my mind while waiting to see the banker was the sizeable crowd he drew to the bank and especially on a Saturday morning. Wow! I thought, if I could learn to draw a crowd like this to my church on Sunday morning, the visit to the bank would serve a dual purpose, especially if I were to be successful in landing the funds with which to buy a car. I determined at that point that one of my opening questions to the banker was going to be "How do you draw such a great crowd to your bank?" I also determined to play heavy on the two words "Your Bank" because I figured that since he was the head man in charge at the bank, he probably owned most of it.

As he would infrequently come to the door with a customer he had finished with and ask, "Who's next?" I got a chance to look at the distinguished banker and the departing customer. It was very amusing to keep score of the ones who obtained their loan as opposed to those who were turned down. The facial expressions of the departing customer made good score keeping a paradise. However, I was puzzled about the non-changing expression on the banker's face as he came through the door with every departing person and ushered the "Who's next" in with him. At this point I had already learned a considerable amount about the man I had to convince to extend a loan to me.

He was well-dressed, shirt and tie I assumed, in his early 50's, wore a crisp West Point type crew cut, with a heavy tinting of gray. His shoulders were extremely broad, and he had the low profile build of a college football halfback. He carried a heavy chew of tobacco in his mouth and spat in the cuspidor near me (no need to look the word up, it's a college word for spittoon!) each time he re-entered the waiting room. I was already armed with enough information about this man to enable me to make at least a favorable opening impression when my turn arrived. I had already learned that there was an unspoken rule in effect in the waiting room, because each time a person left the room (which was always the one in the chair closest to the door), everybody got up and moved up a notch toward the envied chair, closest to the door.

Finally, I was sitting in that chair, and suddenly I found myself as nervous as a long-tailed cat in a room filled with active rocking chairs! I had learned from my advancing predecessor that the illustrious banker's name was Mr. LaRue Parrish, and that he was indeed the president of Adel Banking Company. I would have settled for someone a bit lower on the bank totem pole, but I thought what-the-heck – if you're going to strike out, it may as well be big league. So I was ready to step up to the plate and take my turn at bat. I was nervous with rocking chair fever, but I thought I had selected a bat I could hit with. I suspect that the reader is wondering why this hound is running this rabbit so long, but I want you to see that I'm after a good prize and that I was soon to meet one of the greatest men ever to come into my circle of friendship.

The moment finally arrived and the "Who's next" announced my time at bat. Incidentally, I still wonder why Mr. Parrish wasted his time with this question. He could just as well have nodded to the coveted chair. After the brief introduction, I took my seat in one of the two customer chairs in front of the large prestigious mahogany desk and posed my first question, coming from the inventory of those I had catalogued while in the waiting room.

"Mr. Parrish, I am the young pastor of the new church over on West Fifth Street, and I want you to tell me how you are able to draw such a great crowd to your bank on an early Saturday morning." With a quick smile that revealed a perfect set of teeth, he replied, "All you have to do is tell them you have some money to lend, and if necessary they will break down the door to get to your church!"

Wow! I thought he had given me the covenanted formula, but I didn't have a cent to lend and to worsen the condition I was in his bank attempting to induce him to make me a loan with which to buy a car!

My instincts told me that I had quickly made a friend, and whether I got the loan or not, my time was well spent because I had met a good man who became my friend until the day of his untimely death. Then his son Allen took over his position as bank president and is one of my favorite friends until this date. Oh, incidentally, I forgot to tell you that I was granted the loan, without a credit check. The trusting banker was one who doubtlessly possessed great ability to assess the trustworthiness and character of people in a few brief moments and could make a determination as to whether or not he was willing to extend credit to that person. This was a time that predated the credit bureaus and other worthy suppliers of credit history information. In fact, the entire lending society operated much the same way. There is also a vast mystification about this manner of doing financial business, but the stark reality is that these wise old bankers like Mr. LaRue Parrish had a much better track record than the bankers do today, even with the aid of all the available credit data supplied by the highly sophisticated computer equipment that places it at our fingertips.

This has been quite a written spiel about an entity and its staff which do business in the high seven figure columns bracket and yet spend almost a negative amount on advertising or other means directed at enticing customers into the bank's lobbies and loan waiting rooms. My aim has been multiple. The church I was serving as pastor had no funds to wage an advertising blitz to arouse awareness of its existence and spread the news about the noble reasons embedded in its mandate to reach the lost with the message of the gospel of Jesus Christ. I had learned a great lesson that day at the bank. I only needed to restructure the superb strategy used successfully by the bank – I had to come up with a product or service which would attract the people to come and try this approach which would be the product of my best offering.

The results were a distant cry to the enormous success Mr. Parrish's bank witnessed week after week as hundreds came to test their ability to secure the aid of a loan, doubtless for every purpose under the sun. However, the small missions church which the wonderful Holy Spirit had helped us to found and pastor grew from a very modest beginning under a gospel tent to the second largest church in attendance in Cook County in less that two years' time. I don't think I ever got around to thanking Mr. LaRue Parrish for the great idea his bank shared with me while in the waiting room. There are many times when I reflect on that very special day. With my mind's eye I can still see a short, graying crew cut man come through the office door and walk over very methodically, spit in the cuspidor, and lift his voice to announce his readiness for another customer by saying, "Who's next?"

No waiting room at the office

Unlike other lending institutions, we do not have a waiting room at the Provident office, and yet the number of loan requests on file is seldom under a two-year waiting period. This truth has been a constant source of great concern to me because I live in an incessant awareness that this company is an integral part of the kingdom of God because of its purpose and mission. We are well aware of the fact that the better we help to equip the pastors and churches of this very strategic region of the earth, the more souls they are going to be able to reach with the Gospel of Jesus Christ. We are also aware of the fact that it is indeed the Lord who gives the increases to the churches, but we may be well assured that the most effective ones invariably are going to be those who have been better equipped. Albeit, I am attempting to be as patient as possible until the Lord sees fit to remove the obstacle which hinders the flow of funds to our coffers, which will enable us to make the loans as rapidly as the requests come in.

I've never had a longing to chew tobacco and spit in the cuspidor like my dear old banker friend, but I have surely envied his waiting room and the source of nearly unlimited funds with which he had access. Until that time arrives, I will continue to wait at least with some measure of patience. I have great faith that one day, not too far in the distant future, we will tap into the fountain that never shall run dry!

News travels by the grapevine

There is an old adage which says that news travels through the grapevine. I have always thought that a better title than "grapevine news" could have been applied to identify the best news source on earth. Now mind you, that like other news sources, the grapevine agency carries all kinds of news. However, it is doubtless the most reliable news source on earth when reputable men and women share their experiences. As I indicated in a previous paragraph, Provident has never spent one red cent on advertising through any agency. As unorthodox as it may seem, we have depended entirely on the "grapevine daily news" to carry our message. The unadulterated truth is that it works and is indeed effective!

Now let me tell you how the "Grapevine Daily" works. The agency is as old as the Bible, and this book which is the greatest of books tells us how news traveled back in those primitive days. There is a story in the book of II Kings, chapter five, about a great Syrian captain named Naaman whose life was spared because of some news he obtained through the Syrian grapevine news. The account tells us that Naaman had climbed the ladder of greatness because of his outstanding ability as "Captain of the Host." He must have been something about like America's Chief of the Armed Forces staff. The biblical report tells us that under Captain Naaman's orders, the Syrian army was conducting raids of terror on the Jewish people. On one of these merciless raids, a small Israeli girl, whose name is not even mentioned, was captured and brought to Syria and assigned duty as a personal maid to Naaman's wife. Now you should keep on reading for we are going to hook up to the "Grapevine Daily" in a few minutes!

Naaman had a very serious case of leprosy and was apparently doomed to die. However, this "little maid" became aware of the condition of Mrs. Naaman's husband. The news was out, and everyone was talking about the impending death of the great Syrian general. The little maid had brought with her some good news from her native land. There was a prophet named Elisha back in Israel who was a specialist at handling those hopeless cases. She shared this news with Mrs. Naaman. The grapevine picked up the good news and again a person whose name is not mentioned carried the news of the hour to the king. If you will read the account in verse five, you will notice that the news is characterized by the verbiage "thus and thus, said the maid." Nonetheless it was a message through the grapevine and became the front page edition in the Syrian country. The most important part of the story was that the good news traveled to the king's palace where considerable dispatch occurred, and arrangements were made to get the leprous man to the prophet of God. If you will read chapter five in its entirety, you will learn that after considerable fanfare, Naaman was humbled and received his healing in the disdainful waters of the Jordan river! Remember, the whole thing started with some good news "through the grapevine" in the house of Naaman in the land of Syria.

The grapevine is timely and accurate

I hope the reader will not think I am irreverent through usage of the grapevine slang, but if I am able to find a better word before this treatise goes to press, if it makes it, I'll make the change, and you'll never know about the original beginning of this paragraph. God works in mysterious ways, and some of the greatest achievements in life result from good news that God's people share with one another by "word of mouth." Now that pseudonym should keep you busy for awhile if you care to find out where it came from.

Two great churches started via grapevine news

The pastor of the Overcoming Faith Church in my hometown of Moultrie, Georgia, is one of the most humble and greatest men I have ever known. His name is

Reverend Willie C. Tatum. God has used this man to build one of the most successful black congregations in the entire area.

The church began rather obscurely in the southeast section of the city of Moultrie. An old house just off Ninth Street which was almost unfit for human occupancy was modified to accommodate a growing congregation. Now in order to keep this grapevine thing in perspective, I need to inform you that I have known Willie C. Tatum for a number of years; in fact, several years ago he and I worked at the same meat processing plant in Moultrie. However, I did not know that he had received the call to preach and had become a very competent orator and spiritual leader. The truth is, I did not know that the Overcoming Faith Church even existed.

Now for the introduction to one of the greatest enigmatic miracles I have ever been associated with. Pastor Tatum has a first cousin named Grant who lives in Oakland, California. He is near the age of retirement, and he flies home two or three times each year to renew his family ties and grassroots connections. He had bought a piece of property within a two-mile distance of the home farm where I have lived for more than 30 years. I was not aware that the property sold nor did I know Grant Tatum at the time. My youngest son, John, owns and operates our old family business in Moultrie, which consists of an equipment rental store, a small Yamaha, and a John Deere tractor lawn and garden equipment dealership. Because Grant had bought a small farm acreage, there was the ever pressing need for some equipment with which to cut the grass and till the soil. The proximity of John's business made it convenient for Grant to come in to rent the needed equipment. Through this rental method, he didn't have the problem of storage and upkeep on the equipment. However, he was so well pleased with the performance of the equipment he had rented, he inquired about the availability of purchase and financing of the small John Deere tractor and equipment he had used. Now we all know that it is not always the easiest thing to do for a man to come from California to Georgia and buy some expensive equipment and expect some gullible banker to provide the necessary financing. However, the grapevine communicator has almost always provided the Summerlin family with sound information, so John brought Grant over to my office since he thought he was a good prospect and hopefully I would provide some personal financing. I had been involved with providing financing in part or whole for many of the projects my building firm was involved with. I guess I am somewhat of the making of the great pioneer Daniel Boone. I have often been noted for taking the grapevine swing! Strictly on the basis that Grant Tatum was a cousin of Willie Tatum who was one of the most honorable men I ever knew, I developed interest in the request. I have always made my judgments on the basis of a person's record since they became a Christian. If you were to look deeply into my record before I met Christ, both of our faces would doubtless blush with shame. I am so glad that the provisions of Calvary put all those old blemished records in the sea of God's forgetfulness! I can now say with the old song writer,

"What sins are you talking about?"

Grant Tatum's credit history report supplied the type of information that would almost induce a New York banker to advance a loan in Australia if Grant so requested. Let's cut the monologue now that we understand how the wonderful Holy Spirit made the connections between three people who were to become an integral link in helping a wonderful church come into a state of fruition.

The element of timing

Remember I mentioned timing a bit earlier in this report? The very day that all these elements were being brought together, doubtless, under the leadership of the Holy Spirit, was the exact day that the attorney for a large church in Albany, Georgia, had informed me earlier that they had been blessed greatly and the church had elected to pay the mortgage off in full in a year, which would be about 10 years in advance of the final due date. The amount was well in the six figure count, and on this precise date I was to go to Albany to pick up a cashier's check for the largest amount of money I would ever carry in my life.

Timing often involves routing, and in this case the routing was as mysterious as the other facets of this arrangement. I had finished the loan arrangement for Grant to buy his new tractor and equipment, and since his mini-farm was located between my office and Albany, I decided to drop by and get him to sign the loan papers on the tractor and equipment. As I vividly recall, when I arrived, I spread the note and allied documents out on the hood of my pickup truck (another of my unorthodox manners in doing business) for Grant to sign. It was on a very hot summer day, and the sun had heated the hood to a high degree on Mr. Farenheit's temperature measuring device. As Grant signed the note, I remarked to him that was possibly the hottest note he would ever sign!

As I started to leave (Grant had no knowledge of where I was going nor the purpose for the trip), he asked me if I knew of someone who would be willing to build a church for a very needy congregation. He pointed in the direction where the land was located and informed me that his cousin Willie and his congregation were wanting to build a much needed church building on the newly acquired property. Grant and his family are loyal supporters of the missions effort, and they planned to join the church membership and lend full support upon his retirement which would be only about two years away. The enthusiastic manner that Grant shared the vision for the church was very compelling. I was intrigued by his sincerity and dedication to a sizeable church project of which he was not yet a full partner.

I hastened to leave due to the impending appointment which was a good hour's drive away. While driving away, I assured him that I would give serious consideration to his request. I knew it was not mere coincidence that a good man did not just happen to travel across a nation, to arrive at a special time and present an urgent need where there would be ample funds available in a matter of a few hours.

You will want to hasten to the next chapter for one of the most thrilling reports about how a church plan came together for the Reverend Willie C. Tatum's congregation.

We will remain hooked up to the Grapevine Daily and take another grapevine swing which will diminish Daniel Boone's greatest effort! Please flip the page and get ready for an exciting report.

Oh yeah! I forgot to tell you Mr. Parrish approved my loan, and I bought the prettiest 1957 Chevrolet you have ever laid eyes on.

Chapter Ten

The Weak vs. The Mighty

H ave you ever wondered how churches come into existence? Contrary to the respected opinion of some, the message to a preacher for a church to be built is usually not thundered out in lightning bolts or even a burning bush! The call is usually birthed in the hearts of men and women who are led of the Holy Spirit and possess a desire to help spread the gospel to needy souls. There are a number of ingredients necessary before a church building can be put together. But you can be well assured that at the base of the effort is a person of enormous dedication. He is usually driven by no visible force, and yet his innermost being is ablaze with the Holy Fire. The prophet Jeremiah described the holy phenomenon as being ... "like a ... burning fire shut up in my bones" (Jeremiah 20:19). Regardless of how the person is chosen to do the work of church planting, we can be assured that the vessel opted for the job is likely to be very simple. However, one should not underestimate the potential of a vessel the Lord has selected to advance the gospel mission in a particular location. Many times I have witnessed the "weak things confound the mighty."

The case of the Overcoming Faith Church and the Reverend Willie C. Tatum is a classic example of the kind heavenly Father's choosing one of those weak instruments and through His process of fire make it strong and equal to the assigned task.

The Reverend Tatum is a simple, tall thin man, soft spoken, extremely kind and understanding, and most folks love him the first time they meet him. He has a big winning smile which readily qualifies him for the neighboring job as peanut farmer to President Jimmy Carter. Even though he is not endowed with much formal education, he is a genius at winning friends and influencing people. Dale Carnegie could have devoted several pages of his best seller book on *How to Win Friends and Influence People* to the winsome life of Willie Tatum had they both lived in the same time span. The story of this wonderful man of God could have warmed the pages of Mr. Carnegie's outstanding literary effort.

The call to the gospel ministry is as mysterious as the call of the swallow, or the spawning of the salmon, or even maybe as enigmatic as the instinct of a homing pigeon. Albeit, few people understand when the heavens issue a call to a man, and he responds by taking up the mantle and begins to follow in the direction of a prescribed post of duty. The Lord's choice of Willie C. Tatum doubtless would have been questioned by some of the more learned and astute crowd! Fortunately, there was no credentialing committee nor governing church body to ascertain the presence or absence of the desired qualities for men of the cloth. His response to the call was answered by a willingness and dedication to preach the gospel and lead mankind to know the Lord Jesus Christ as savior. While it is not the intention of the writer to downplay nor belittle the importance of well organized church group organizations and their inherent right to properly credential candidates, I do share the conviction that an army of Christian soldiers have been kept from duty in the harvest fields because of stringent criteria and rules that deemed them unacceptable for the high positions of church leadership. Those, who aspire to impose and uphold the uncompromising high educational standards and training for ministerial candidates, would do well to read the many biblical accounts where God issued a call to man. These obedient servants came forward when called and became a blazing torch of evangelism for the sake of the Christian gospel.

A small group of friends and family who shared the conviction that Willie Tatum had received the Master's call responded by helping him to locate and refurbish an old house in the city of Moultrie for the purpose of church worship. The old building was crudely shaped as a worship facility, and within a few weeks the attendance grew from less than a baker's dozen to a full house crowd with attendance of almost 100 people. I have known scores of preachers with college degrees and ample seminary training who did not accomplish as much in a lifetime as Pastor Tatum did in a few months of labor. In addition to the sound growth in attendance, the small congregation was able to save more than $20,000 to be used to help them acquire a decent church building for worship purposes and to house the steadily increasing group of dedicated church followers.

Again, a local banking institution was happy to accommodate the church savings account and an attractive checking account, but their reaction to numerous request for a loan to help with financing a church facility was as cold as a welldigger's foot! At this juncture the church, through a special meeting of divine implications, sought help from Provident to finance their building loan requirements. This meeting between Grant Tatum and the writer was described in complete details in the previous chapter. Suffice it to say that the meeting was very fruitful and in a matter of a few days plans were underway to develop a complete set of church building plans which were to bear an identity that would compliment Pastor Tatum's great congregation.

Provident develops a great plan image

What the name of Tom Houston has come to be to the roasted peanut industry of Tom's roasted peanuts or the name of Frito-Lay to the potato chip industry, the name Provident is developing in corresponding character to the church building world. We have on file a sizeable inventory of church plans which usually, with minor alterations, can be shaped to fit any size church congregation from fewer than 100 to several thousand. The availability of this large plans inventory is made available to any who may wish to use this great service. This generous offering by our company represents a savings of several thousand dollars to the church body who avails themselves of this chivalrous gesture.

Pastor Tatum was quick to seize the opportunity to develop a special set of plans to be used as a guide for erecting a church building with a strong countryside appearance. The building was to be built on a sizeable lot about four miles from the city of Moultrie, Georgia, in the agricultural heart of the southland. In a time frame of less than three months, the plans were modified by the building construction engineer and were ready for the sizeable task of translating from the dream to the real thing. The plans called for a 3300-plus square foot building to be erected on a two-acre tract of land. The projected cost of the building was $150,000. This figure included a deep well as a water source, a sizeable septic tank sewer project, and 600 square foot building located near the church to house lawn and garden equipment and other church storage. All of this was in the offering for a price of less than $160,000. The package also included a small John Deere tractor and allied equipment which was to be used to cut and groom the landscape of several acres of property owned by the church.

Ground breaking begins

Have you ever wondered where the idea of the ground breaking ceremony came from and the use of the golden shovel? My limited research has not revealed a clue. Upon suggesting the idea to Pastor Tatum, he was elated. It would be a great time to announce publicly the plans of the church to build a gospel lighthouse in a real growth area of Colquitt County where a heavy concentration of people who were sympathetic with the mission of the Overcoming Faith Church had begun to relocate and build.

The news was considered good public relations by the local newspaper, and they eagerly supplied a news

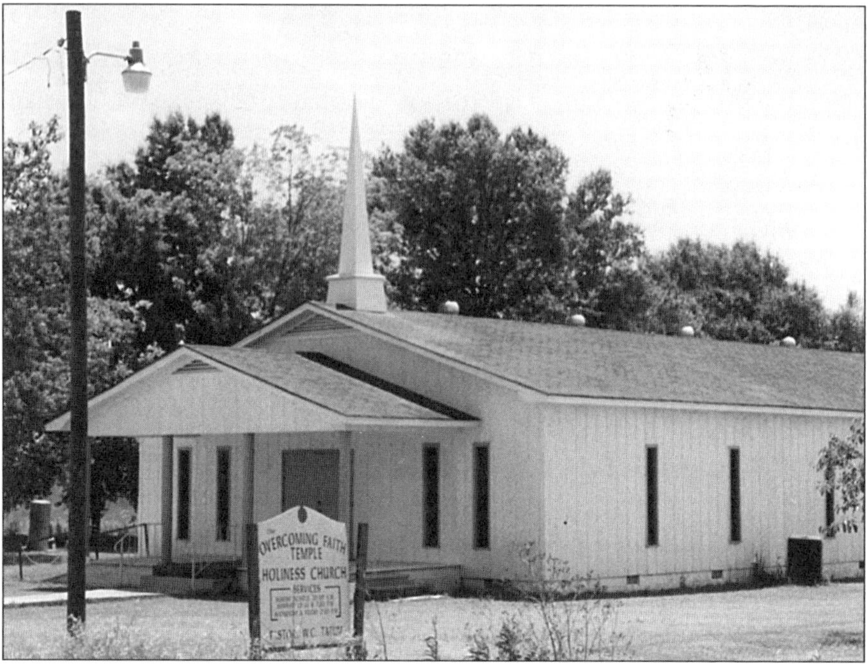

Overcoming Faith Temple Church, Moultrie, Georgia

reporter to gather the story of an unlikely local man who had met with measurable success in the church growth world. The time was announced for a Sunday afternoon gathering where an impressionable crowd gathered to share the joy of the thrilling experience of digging with the golden shovels! Of course no one in the Provident group nor the willing workers band of Pastor Tatum's growing church had the money to buy the gold plated shovels like those which are housed in the elaborate foyers and vestibules of distinguished landmark buildings. However, I found out that a 99-cent can of Rose's spray paint would produce six gold-plated shovels! Of course, I'm talking about a poor man's version of the frame-worthy tool which sold for less than $4 at the local hardware store. Anyway, no one could tell the difference in the news story in the newspaper which was printed in black and white!

The blessing of the cost plus approach

There is not a better way economically to accost a building project effort than through the basic cost method plus a percentage profit fee for the builder. Of course this is only possible when there is present an abundance of integrity, honesty and a truckload of willingness to expend every possible effort to build a building at the lowest possible cost. There was no doubt that all of these necessary ingredients were present because the people involved in this effort had been up to bat several times before and were capable and ready to flex their muscle of experience to raise up a new gospel lighthouse!

Within a time frame of less than four months, the lovely wood frame building, capped with a tall spiral type steeple was readied for official dedication. As the word spread about the great dedicatorial service, the crowds began to gather to share the crowning success of a very poor, uneducated black man whose greatest asset was a dedicated life to the kingdom of God. He was able under the leadership of the wonderful Holy Spirit to help scores of people to know Jesus Christ as a personal savior.

I was deeply humbled to be asked to deliver the dedicatorial address to a crowd large enough to twice fill the 200-seat sanctuary. As I surveyed a portion of the enthusiastic crowd which was able to gather in the auditorium for a seat, I was able to catch a glimpse of the faces of those who had been delivered from sin and had taken up the cross of obedience to follow their Savior. Many of them I had known for several years. They came from almost every walk of life. Many of them were like the man seated on the platform before he came to know Jesus. He was shackled with a load of guilt and sin. Poverty and misery were constant companions. As I viewed the countenances of those dear people, I was able to respond in kindred spirit because the blood of Jesus Christ is still able to make the vilest sinner clean! The spirit of Christ had bonded us with the spirit of brotherhood. None of the things we were witnessing on this red-letter day would have been possible without the unifying provisions of the Cross of Calvary!

The arrival of Reverend Israel Blake

Among the host of several hundred guests sharing the victory celebration was another of the sons of Abraham. He was obviously a top graduate from the University of Smiles because every muscle in his body blended in harmony to produce an Olympic-style smile. He was cheerful, effervescent and sported a parlance as smooth as a well-graded country road. The manner in which he gripped my hand, combined with other well coordinated body language, let me know that he was a child of God and that he wanted to become my friend. As far I was concerned, he was already aboard!

He very enthusiastically invited me to visit his church in Thomasville, Georgia, a lovely city located a score and eight miles south of Moultrie. The charming city is renowned for its voluminous production of every variety of roses. In fact, it is called the City of Roses. The invitation was extended with a strong macedonian urgency, "Come over to Macedonia and help us." I knew immediately that it was not just the voice of Pastor Blake, but it was a call from the Holy Spirit who has also been my special friend for almost half a century! I immediately answered the call by giving a time when I would call at the Mission Station in the Rose City.

As I recall it was on a Wednesday night in the month of August in 1991 when my wife Myrtle and I rode down to the charming city. Every street we traveled was well manicured, and many of the popular prickly shrubs continued to support a myriad of the pedestal supported flowers of beauty. My wife, who is a great lover of flowers and more than an amateur flower gardener in her own right, was awed by the late autumn display by the rose family.

When we arrived at the address given by Pastor Blake, the street on which the mission station was located had not received the same meticulous gardening care as the main thoroughfares. The building was in an ill state of repair, but neither the state of repair nor the location diminished from the fervent prayer service which was in progress inside the converted frame house. A greeter, who was mindful of our announced arrival, was waiting outside the door to signal the arrival of a guest who might be able to help them begin the exciting journey of a church building project. The initial evidence was convincing that no congregation in America was in more desperate need of a new worship facility than the House of Prayer Church, led by the Reverend Israel Blake. I am noted for attaching nicknames to church congregations, and on that hot night of August I told the greeter that I had come to visit Pastor Blake and the Children of Israel! He grinned from ear to ear and flashed a giant smile, as he pointed toward the old antique eight panel door and said, "This is the way, Sir!"

More convincing evidence

When our greeter opened the door, it seemed that a rush of the heavenly atmosphere charged in our direction which caused a spell of holy goose pimples to run up and down my spine. The service in progress within the crudely fashioned auditorium caused an even greater thrill! The sight was in my view much like I have envisioned the upper room meeting described by the writer of the book of Acts. The prayer altars were filled with earnest souls seeking to know the mind and will of a forgiving Jesus. The open area between the rows of crudely-made pews and the lectern was filled with folks lying on the floor. Many of them were speaking in a language which was totally unfamiliar to my English ear, but I had no trouble recognizing that it was coming from a power higher than the highest summits of mankind, and I knew that the implications bore a message from heaven. I facetiously queried the pastor about this strange phenomenon by asking, "What is the meaning of all this?" He replied, "I don't rightly know, but some folk call it the Holy Ghost!"

It appeared to me that the heavenly Father had poured forth His holy anointing upon the waiting believers in the form of the infilling of the Holy Spirit! I am much like Pastor Blake – the only thing I know is what the Bible and some folks call it. I know one thing for sure, I was about to freeze in the middle of one of the hottest nights in south Georgia when the temperature was near the 100-degree mark, allowing no factor for the amount of body heat generated in the small room by a group of folks who were expending every effort possible to help the waiting disciples of Christ to make connection with the power of the Holy Spirit!

My wife and I left the "red hot" meeting with our hearts aglow with the heavenly flame from the gentle spirit which was being poured forth in the small room where people worship the heavenly Father. As we drove back in the direction of our hometown, my wife noticed that I had not gathered the voluminous amount of information that I usually gather or ask for at every meeting of this nature. I replied to her that I already decided to ask the board to approve this loan. If ever in my life I have witnessed the power of God and felt an unction to approve a loan, I felt not only a green light to lend approval to their request, but I sensed an urgency to get the building project moving forward as soon as possible.

The absence of committee hassle

During the time I was building the last church I was to pastor, there was an abundance of committees and individuals who gave more than ample time to express their pleasure with the many facets of the building project. The project was not a small one; funds were in short supply and a number of us donated thousands of hours of labor to erect the sizeable worship facility within an affordable monthly mortgage payment. My patience had grown thin from the near daily contact from those who came by to lend their expert ideas or desires. At times they left a truck load of both.

During this time, I was working a regular day shift doing carpentry work for eight hours, a short night shift with some dedicated volunteers in addition to the regular pastoral duties of a sizeable congregation. The burden of preparation and delivery of at least three sermons each week was a guarantee of a full workweek. At a point during this time, I was in deep need of some good intervention to break the lengthy humdrum of labor. One of the many kind and considerate members of the church came by one day and brought a lovely little desk plaque which read, "FOR GOD SO LOVED THE WORLD THAT HE DIDN'T SEND A COMMITTEE." I am so glad that He didn't, but rather chose to send the Son of God! That timely and meaningful little plaque remains on the credenza in my office until today!

Now for the main point of this somewhat lengthy dissertation.

Old home of House of Prayer Church, Thomasville, Georgia

Rev. & Mrs. Israel Blake

New House of Prayer where great revival began

He didn't send a committee

The congregation of Pastor Israel Blake had complete confidence in his leadership abilities. Consequently, they extended to him the complete authority to address my decisions regarding the building project. Obviously, he conferred with his staff regularly to obtain their input and wisdom, but he was indeed vested with complete authority and responsibility for the building process.

I suppose this is one of the reasons that I have enjoyed the home missions type building so very much. This is the area of my greatest expertise, and it is also the reward of being able to work with men and women who have so recently heard from heaven and know what the mind of Christ is for them and their infant congregations. The absence of numerous committees and some self-appointed delegates makes the work of the Lord's business much easier and meaningful. I am confident that these well-intentioned folk mean to do well, but all of us know that too much can cause delay and many times waste. I have seen committees hassle and argue over the color of carpet for a sanctuary for 90 days! I often wonder how many souls have been lost as a result of our "over attention" to trivial matters. Pastor Blake had told me before we started the work on the new church that the Lord had told him that the carpet was to be red. Oh yeah, the congregation agreed with him 100 percent!

The beautiful brick veneered building, with a vaulted cathedral-type ceiling in the auditorium, coupled with four classrooms and a large social hall was completed in a few brief months and was ready for dedication occupancy a few days before Christmas in the year of our Lord 1991.

A baptismal service not soon to be forgotten

I was not privileged to be in the first series of meetings held in the new church, but some minor unfinished construction matters necessitated my return to Pastor Blake's church on a Monday following the weekend Yuletide services. The matters I came to see about were in the social hall. Upon entering in the pastor's presence, I noticed there was considerable water on the vinyl covered floors. I inquired about the matter, thinking we had a minor plumbing problem. The pastor responded in a croupy-type voice, which I knew was the result of fervent heated preaching, that the Lord's children were so thrilled and excited when a number came forward for water baptism in the new aqua colored indoor baptistry. A number were baptized and shouted through the "troubled waters" (Pastor Blake's words in quotes) and knocked some of the holy water out of the pool onto the floor!

This may seem a bit strange or unorthodox to some who may read this, but understand that most of these dear people had never been in a church service before where all the great conveniences of church worship are available for the first time. Especially, when suddenly all of these luxuries are yours and the Lord has provided an atmosphere conducive to their use. I have no trouble in understanding the exuberance exhibited by Pastor Blake's flock. I wish many times for the Lord to "trouble the waters" in many of our churches who have lost their joy and spiritual enthusiasm. A little water spilled on the floor could be a healthy sign that the Lord's blessing and approval are upon our works of obedience.

A revival that follows

Shortly after the completion of the church, a revival began that was to almost double the size of the congregation. The revival meeting, under the leadership of Pastor Blake and other evangelists whom they had invited to offer their words from the Lord, resulted in the conversion of 82 souls in less than one month of continuous services. Among these were a number of children and young people who were to help impact a large area of Thomas County for Christ. Many of them were from alcohol and drug-influenced homes where the tender shepherding care of a caring church like Reverend Israel Blake offered was totally unknown. The house-to-house search by a caring congregation paid a dividend so great that it will require the heavenly computers to calculate. It is only those who know the value of a soul who will be able to relate to the contribution the small Thomasville church has made to the Kingdom of God.

The effects of the missionary efforts of this church upon communities in neighboring counties will be discussed in a later chapter if there is room for continuation of so great a testimony. The fact that Provident was an integral part of the House of Prayer ministry and many others should make all of us who are connected with this great ministry of church financing extremely proud and grateful to God that we have been a small part. It could be said that we, like Aaron and Hur, have been the ones who have sat on the rock and held up the hands of Israel while the church He leads conquers Satan's strongholds and reaps the

**Front and rear view of House of Prayer Church
Bainbridge, Georgia**

**Formerly the old Bainbridge Methodist Church
Over 100 years old**

ripened harvest for the Master! From my personal point of view, there have been no real sacrifices, only opportunities to assist a man or woman who has heard from the throne room and has been courageous enough to answer, "Here am I [Lord], send me," Isaiah 6:8.

I feel sure you will hasten to move to the next chapter where we will share some of the most exciting testimonies about some wonderful women who, like Deborah, Mary, Martha, Priscilla, and numerous others who have heard from God, provided sound leadership in their times. No attempt has been made to separate the gender contributions. Old mother time under spirit leadership brought these leaders into fruition. Their contributions toward advancing the kingdom of God will thrill and excite you, I'm sure. Please read on!

Chapter Eleven

Torchbearers of a Special Kind

I doubt if many men who have been torchbearers for Christ have fully understood and appreciated the role played by the special women whom the Lord has chosen and called to gospel ministry. The fact that they labor under many disadvantages is not broadly understood, and the unwise even dare to criticize their efforts. The purpose of this chapter is not intended to gain sympathy or approval for these great spiritual leaders but rather to explain that their assignment has also been difficult and in many cases the labor burden made greater simply because they were women. I must hasten to tell you that these warriors of the cross have not asked for a place in this treatise but those who read would be much less enriched if I failed to include their distinguished contribution. So here goes the story!

Anderson Greatly Impacted by Lady Pastor

The city of Anderson is located a few miles from the Georgia state line just off Interstate Highway 85. The city is populated with a balanced mixture of the caucasian race, blacks, and other minority races. The area is highly industrialized, and the job market offers a variety of highly-skilled, well-paying jobs for the working class people.

Old Wesleyan Pastorium, South Main Street, Anderson, SC

Front view of old Wesleyan Church owned and occupied by Gospel Tabernacle Church.

Rev. Velma Williford and husband Claude, Pastors

Old house next door to sanctuary
now owned by Gospel Tabernacle

Fellowship Hall, Gospel Tabernacle

This category of people is doubtless the heart and soul of America. They also are the mainstream of our churches and offer the church its greatest opportunity for evangelization and advancement.

It was here in Anderson, South Carolina, in the mid-70's that Velma Williford and her husband Claude were converted and answered the call to the gospel ministry. Although Claude will categorically deny any call to preach the gospel, he is doubtless one of the finest and able men in the area. He is extremely supportive of his wife's ministry and pastoral functions. Their families have lengthy and well-reputed genealogies and are well respected and loved by the people in Anderson County.

They began their ministry in a crudely-shaped facility without many of the conveniences other churches and religious groups enjoyed. However, these inconveniences were mild when compared to the flame and fire of the Holy Spirit which was ablaze in their hearts. Their efforts of labor in the ripened harvest field were rewarded by a number of conversions. These new converts were attracted to the missions effort by the persuasive work of the Holy Spirit and the sound enthusiastic messages of the cross and the blood of the Lamb, offered by the anointed preaching of Pastor/Evangelist Velma Williford. The church mission effort began with a zero membership, but within a few months the small facility was too small to house the growing congregation.

A new work in Greenwood, South Carolina

A few months after beginning the mission work in Anderson, the Holy Spirit led Pastor Williford to start a

Old elementary school now the home of Zion Tabernacle
Church Greenwood, SC. (Front and side views)

Historic gazebo, Greenwood, SC

Rear view of elementary school now occupied by Zion Tabernacle, Greenwood, SC

Side view of elementary school, Zion Tabernacle, Greenwood, SC

Side view of historic gazebo

kindred work in the city of Greenwood, South Carolina. The lovely city with a population of approximately 30,000 offered a challenge for the church to broaden its mission and enlist others to labor in the ripened harvest fields. The story of this work is another work of miracles and will be shared later in this chapter, but to mention this breathtaking effort will help to establish some order of chronological sequence about how God used a lady Pastor/Evangelist to do a work that has been achieved by few. She gained the respect of men and women alike as she blazed the mission trails in search of the lost and dying.

A contention which spawned growth

The book of Acts contains a brief story (Acts 15:36-41) about a very private affair between Paul and Barnabas which the Holy Spirit urged Luke to record. The event was doubtless not the most popular thing these giants of faith ever did, but God chose to use this unpleasant experience to double his missionary strength. The element which divided the great men of faith was whether John Mark should be permitted to rejoin the missionary team from which he had defected some time before. Unable to resolve the division, the two men went in different directions. Barnabas chose John Mark, and Paul tabbed Silas as a new partner, respectively. We do not have to wonder what was lost for the kingdom of God, for the results speak for themselves.

A similar incident happened a few years after the Willifords began their ministry in Anderson County. A conflict developed with the parent body of the church organization of which the Anderson church was associated. The matter could not be resolved; therefore an impasse evolved which resulted in the censure and dismissal of Pastor Velma Williford. The vast majority of the congregation was sympathetic with the pastor and chose to follow her in another new missions effort in the city of Anderson. There were about 100 people without a building to worship in and to house them from the winter elements.

Provident becomes a friend

An acquaintance had developed earlier between the writer and the Williford family which proved to be extremely beneficial at this time of great crisis. The small congregation was unable to remove any of the furnishings from the previous worship facility nor one cent of money which was in the church coffers. Most members were working type folk and lived from week to week on their meager earnings, unable to save anything for a stormy day. Being suddenly thrust into the storm was unpleasant and uncomfortable to say the least. There was not enough cash money in the sum total of the membership's possession to even make the down payment on a piece of ground, not to mention the exorbitant cost of building a new facility.

Pastor Williford contacted me and asked that I come up to encourage and if at all possible to help the destitute flock to obtain a worship facility. In the meantime Pastor Williford had located an empty store building, which they were able to secure on a short-term rental basis. I sensed an urgency about the situation and accepted an invitation to visit and speak in the store-made-church facility. Upon arrival, I noticed that the check-out counters were not busy nor were the cash registers ringing up the receipts. However, the hallejuahs and amens were ringing in a manner that would have silenced the market place!

The small building was packed to capacity, and already new faces were present among the transplanted congregation. The message was loud and clear. The resolve was visible that this church would weather the storm and emerge stronger than ever before. I am of the candid opinion that adversity is not the arch enemy of the church that most of us have envisioned it to be. I know of few cases where the church has not risen to greater heights and strengths after the furious invasion of adversity. A real victory awaits all who are willing to stand against those forces who are destined to interrupt and impede the progress of the Church of Jesus Christ.

The need for open eyes

There is a great story in II Kings 6:15-17 that everyone should read, especially if he is facing a trial or test, and there is no apparent way of escape. The story is so closely related to the adventurous journey of the Anderson congregation that I wish to quote it for a reminder and admonition to all of us who may face adversity now or at some future date.

"And when the servant of the man of God arose early and went out, there was an army, surrounding the city with horses and chariots. And his servant said to him, 'Alas, my master! What shall we do?' So he answered, 'Do not fear, for those who are with us are more than those who are with them.' And Elisha prayed, and said, 'Lord, I pray, open his eyes that he may see.' Then the Lord opened the eyes of the young man, and he saw. And behold, the mountain was full of horses and chariots of fire all around Elisha."

You may not find a mountain filled with horses and chariots, but I am totally confident that you will see or find exactly what God has in mind for you in any given situation.

In the case of the flock of Pastor Williford, when they were able to focus on the answer more than the need, the Lord showed them a beautiful complete facility on South Main Street about two blocks from downtown. The wonderful Wesleyan Methodist folks a few months earlier had seen the need to relocate their downtown church congregation to a greater growth area on one of the main traffic arteries and consolidate two congregations into a new modern more spacious worship facility. They had offered for sale the downtown facility which included a lovely brick church with a two-story educational facility, a three-bedroom frame house, in need of some repair, together with a masonry dining and kitchen facility in excellent state of repair. All of these buildings were situated on three large building lots on South Main Street, a mere hefty stone's throw from the downtown historic district.

All of these accommodations were offered to the "Tabernacle of Faith" (name chosen for the new congregation) for the unbelievably low price of $90,000. Oh yeah, there was the added bonus of all the furnishings in the old church complete with pews and furniture! All of this the Lord had in reserve for a congregation if they would open their eyes to behold the vast provision!

Contacts were made with the governing body of the Wesleyan church, and they were very pleased to participate in a financing aid agreement with Provident to finance the complete facility for the Tabernacle of Faith Church, led by Pastor Velma Williford. In a matter of a few days, the buzz of saws, the smell of new paint, and the united hum of a grateful congregation were heard by all who came by to help or visit.

Many other prayers answered

The burden for the church to prepare and furnish free meals to needy and underprivileged children had been upon the Willifords' hearts for a long time. A facility to prepare these meals and other facilities to involve the youth to get them off the streets and away from drug and alcohol exposure had been the constant prayer of these visionary warriors of the cross. Now suddenly, as the call for help was given to the Provident family, we were able to help this congregation move into an affordable church plant, embracing all the things they had prayed for months. The Lord provided them with everything they needed!

I was invited back a few weeks later to speak at the dedicatorial service, and the fruits of labor from every sector of this church facility were evident. The sanctuary was packed to capacity. The social building was stuffed with old-time home cooks who would have made Chef Boy-ar-dee look like a rookie at a cooking convention!

There were at least 50 new children present and many of them from underprivileged homes. You could not tell the difference, for new clothes and shoes were provided by a caring and sharing church. All the children resembled the children of a king! Their eyes were aglow with the love of Jesus, and their beaming faces reflected the change that only the Cross of Calvary can make.

I would be less than kind if I failed to share with you about one of the most moving experiences of my life. My wife and I were called into the church office before the morning service began to behold the gifted creations by master seamstresses who were members of the church. Some of the church leaders had earlier canvassed the neighborhood in search of children who were kept away from church due to the lack of decent clothing. The search netted a number of boys and girls who fit into the below-poverty category. Among these were 12 little girls ranging in ages from 5 to 13. The pastor secured the necessary cloth and accessories, and gifted church seamstresses made lovely dresses complete with other necessary clothing where these little girls would not feel out of style and place on the approaching Easter Sunday!

My eyes welled up with tears as I looked at my wife who already had tears coursing down her cheeks as we viewed a church that really cared! I will always be grateful to God who saw fit to place me in a position of leadership with our company, Provident Investment Corporation. From this stance I can view our organization in its greatest performance as a vessel to provide funds and financing for churches that are in the business of ministering to the lost and unfortunate. May we never lose our compassion and dedication to all people and all churches!

As members and stockholders of Provident, we can be justly proud of our ministry and mission. There was not one single lending institution in all of Anderson County, South Carolina, who was willing to risk a loan to one of the most spiritual and humanitarian institutions in their populace. We have made a total of three loans to the Tabernacle of Faith Church since the first loan to buy the old Methodist church buildings. Since then we have provided funds to purchase a house and lot adjacent to the church on the back side which fronts on another street. This building is to be renovated and used as a pregnancy crisis center to assist young teenage girls in coping with one of the most flagrant and growing problems in America. The girls are being led to know Christ as a personal savior, and the church is building a lasting friendship in these young unwed mothers. They are being taught how to cope and rebound from this embarrassing and humiliating experience. Many are responding in a positive manner and are going on to live productive and rewarding lives as members of a church who cared enough to stop and pick them up, while others had passed them by.

Recently a loan was made to this church to purchase a beautiful three-bedroom brick house which is located on the south side of the church with adjoining lots. This property has been remodeled by the working membership of the church and is used for housing for the elderly. The rental income will defray the loan cost, and in a few years the church will own property on South Main Street which is now worth more than three times the purchase price. We salute Pastor Williford and her dedicated and visionary congregation for outstanding Christian ministry in a ripened harvest field.

The Greenwood story resumed

You remember that we mentioned earlier in this chapter about a missionary effort Pastor Williford began in the city of Greenwood. This lovely city, located approximately 25 miles from Anderson, is not quite as industrialized as Anderson but is deep and enriched in culture and history. Many of the old antebellum homes and civic buildings remain and cause one to question why General Sherman and his vast army of destruction allowed these buildings to stand. It may have been that God foresaw that the Willifords were going to need the old library building to begin a new missionary work many years later. Therefore, He caused the advancing army to see these buildings as no threat to his mission and spared many, including the old library building, as a place the Lord would choose to establish a soul-saving station almost 125 years later! It is amazing when we are able to witness the foresight of God!

The contention we discussed earlier between the parent church body and Pastor Williford obviously involved the work at Greenwood since she was the pastor. The congregation made a similar decision and left a very comfortable church building which had replaced the old historic library building. Another vacant store building, which was in a very ill state of repair and heavily infested with rodents in terrifying proportion, was located for worship purposes.

Upon answering the pastor's call to come and assist in establishing some direction for the new work, I ministered to my first congregation when the large rats roamed about, apparently attempting to understand why such an enthusiastic crowd had come to share their building. This scene was one of the most heart-rending situations I have ever witnessed. My personal experiences as a home missions pastor over a span of 40 years had covered canvas tents, leaky roofs, and foul odors from unoccupied buildings but never anything of the magnitude the Greenwood congregation was facing.

My immediate response was that we would help this needy congregation just as soon as suitable properties could be located. I had no doubt that our board of directors would lend support to my worthwhile effort to get this congregation of approximately 75 people into a decent worship structure. In the meantime God moved upon the heart of a pastor on the other side of the city of Greenwood to share their church building with the needy flock. The time and dates for services were adjusted to accommodate both congregations. A strong affinity developed between these people as a result of sharing in time of need. This healthy relationship exists until this date and doubtless will continue.

A repeat of the "Open Your Eyes" experiences

A member of Pastor Williford's congregation lived in an area of Greenwood where the Grinnel Corporation had a large mill to produce fabric-related products. The complex included a spacious office building, together with a sound three-story structure which had been used as a school for the children of parents who worked in the mill facility. Automated equipment which produced several times the amount of yarn and thread fabrics produced by the old man-assisted machines had been installed in other modern and strategically located facilities. Thereby, the wisdom of the management of the Grinnel Corporation decided to close the Greenwood facility and offer the buildings for sale.

An alert church member who lived in the area heard about the offering and availability of these buildings and saw the possibilities and potential of this property as a site for their church. She immediately contacted Pastor Williford and arranged for an examination of the main office building and old school building. Pastor Velma and her husband Claude came immediately and saw the potential of the sound masonry constructed buildings. Both buildings were offered as one tract for the amazingly low price of $80,000. Either building was well worth the asking price.

The old office building needed some cosmetic repair and would also require extensive modification before it could be used as a church facility. The pastor knew that either of the historic buildings could serve the purpose of a church facility, and she hastily contacted the Provident office for help in investigating the possibility of acquiring one or both of these buildings and also to estimate the cost of renovating the structures for the intended purpose of church worship.

Being totally mindful of the urgency of the situation, I solicited the assistance of a brother who was elected as an advisor to the board of directors. The two of us made the lengthy journey from Moultrie, Georgia, to Greenwood to lend advice and counsel to the anxious pastor. Exuberance would be an understatement of the vaulted attitude exhibited by the pastor and others who met us in the early morning. We inspected the buildings and made a rather hasty decision as to the possibility of extending a loan to purchase the property and also defray the renovating costs. The office building was extremely attractive with a paved parking lot, but the school building with almost 8,000 square feet of floor space was equally attractive. This building was also situated on almost a square block of prime city property with a separate octagonal gazebo bearing historic significance. I was informed that the city of Greenwood had interest in this property in order to preserve its historical image. The only problem we saw was that the Grinnel Corporation was unwilling to divide the properties; therefore, we verbally committed to buy the property as offered, totally aware of the fact that either piece of property could be sold later for an amount near the total market figure.

A loan closing that sparkled

Arrangements were made with a local law firm to do the title search and other necessary legal work prior to the loan closing. The lengthy process was completed, and a date was announced for the loan closing. I joined the anxious church party which was authorized to officially sign for the church corporation in spacious law offices in downtown Greenwood for the momentous loan closing. Most folk who know me are fully aware of the fact that I am not given much to elaborate dress and many times arrive in work clothes, when in the judgment of some, a suit would be more appropriate. On one occasion when I had to crawl under a building in a stylish Botany 500 suit to check a building prior to loan closing, I learned that work clothes were a pleasant alternative.

Nevertheless as I had joined the church group, the lovely young receptionist had determined that I was apparently a member of the group and continued to stall the loan closing waiting for the arrival of the banker. After a delay of several minutes, Pastor Williford stepped up to the reception window and inquired as to the reason for the delay. The young lady replied, "We are waiting for the arrival of the banker." The pastor informed the somewhat shocked legal secretary that the man over there in the blue denim overalls and blue shirt is the man who would write the check. The secretary responded by saying, "Oh, I'm sorry, I thought he was here to sign the note!"

We were hastily seated in the conference room where an official from the Grinnel Corporation was seated with the attorney. Both men looked somewhat puzzled as the attorney shared with us about a problem the lending institution had regarding a mortgage they held on the property. As I remember, the banking firm held a note on the properties for an amount greater than the selling price and was unwilling to release the claim for the amount of sale.

The pastor inquired about the possibility of dividing the property and selling the old school building separately. The seller was mindful that the office building carried a greater market value than the old school building and hastily seized the opportunity and agreed to sell the school building and almost a city block of property to the church for $40,000! The law office atmosphere almost erupted into a church atmosphere as the Lord miraculously worked out the situation for the church to obtain what it really needed, and the sellers retained the other property which was more valuable from their point of view. The necessary changes were made by the attorney and in less than two hours both seller and the new property owners walked out of the building in a mind frame of victory! I later told Pastor Williford that she was attempting to buy a mountain with too many chariots, and the Lord required her to permit the unselfish company to keep at least one chariot for themselves!

Building renovated and occupied

An additional $20,000 was approved for renovating the old school building, making the total loan for the project $60,000. When you stop to calculate the cost at less than $7 per square foot, it is hard to believe that the Greenwood church family received such an enormous gift from the hand of the Lord and other sympathetic people.

To give the reader something to really ponder and boggle the mind, that figure includes a modern kitchen and dining hall with nearly 2,800 square feet of floor space on the first floor. The second floor, which is near ground level on the front street, contains a new auditorium which will seat almost 200 people and four classrooms and church offices. The third floor with similar floor space is total classroom space for a Sunday School that may grow to more than 200 without being crowded. I continue to feel a shout as I write this brief history a few years after the miracle!

Chapter Twelve

A Record Loan to a Deserving Church

Have you ever wished one of those heavenly fairies (if there is such a creature) could touch your eyes and enable you to see the massive network of the heavenly hosts as they hasten about the heavens performing the will of the heavenly father? I have! It would be a wondrous sight to watch these angelic hosts as they travel around at the speed of light, delivering messages, moving people from place to place, enabling them to mature and get in the right spot at the right time. The lives of people in many ways resemble the flowering plants and trees. These magnificent creations in the plant world almost go unnoticed until they burst forth with their flowering magic and intrinsic beauty. Most of us pay little to no attention to the seeding and growth process. We seem to wait for the spectacular before we offer our oohs and ahs to congratulate the beauty of the outgrowth.

Nothing has more beauty than a person whom God, through the power of the Holy Spirit and the growth process, has brought into spiritual delectation. Here, too, we are unable to see the years of fitting, growth, and discipline before a person steps forth into maturity. The person is now ready for the assignment that only divine perogatives have been privy to.

A special person worthy of literary exploitation is the Reverend Larry D. Manning who resides in the city of Valdosta, Georgia. Pastor Manning's childhood training coupled with a 20-plus year career with the United States Air Force carried him through global training and travel. During most of this time, he was being groomed and trained to begin one of the fast growing minority churches in the Valdosta/Lowndes County area. He had received the call to gospel ministry a few years before his military retirement. An all-wise God had all of this planned years before, and at the precise time He would cause this young man to step forth and to found and begin New Life Baptist Church. The church officially began April 28, 1991, in the home of Deacon Ralph Roberson with a small congregation of approximately 50 people who were visionary and wished to help spread the gospel through a new home mission effort.

A small house located on Mildred Street in Valdosta was secured for the initial home of the New Life congregation. It was there that they began their ministry and acts of power. The small house was converted into a large room sanctuary. In a matter of a few months the building, with a seating capacity of fewer than 100, was experiencing double status crowds with more than 200 people in attendance at Sunday services.

The church leadership, being mindful of the crowded condition, was unable to convince the local lending authorities to make them a loan with which to build a comfortable building as a place of worship. At this juncture when there was not one square foot of space to put another person, the

Good Lord swung "old grapevine control" in the direction of the New Life Church. A member of Pastor Henry Wright II's congregation had been talking to a member of Pastor Manning's congregation, telling of a prayer answering enigma and how Provident had been a godsend for them.

We had built a sizeable church for Pastor Wright in 1987 in Valdosta. A part of that great story was shared in an earlier chapter. The good news was shared with Pastor Manning, and he immediately dispatched a financial committee to the Provident office in Moultrie in search of a helping hand.

The initial meeting revealed that the committee, representing the church body, was in possession of a set of plans with which they were not totally comfortable. A series of meetings were held later between the Provident leadership and the church committee, attempting to come up with a plan that the church body could afford and at the same time accommodate the basic needs of a growing congregation.

The New Life leadership consisted of Pastor Larry Manning and a deacon board of 17 dedicated men who were spirit-filled. They were focused in unison to convince the Provident committee that they were credit worthy people who were in desperate need of a larger facility. The fact that they had already saved $100,000 and had all their property paid for including a sizeable lot for the proposed structure was not a hindrance toward helping them!

I have a personal unwritten policy about visiting the churches where the company is considering making new loans. I usually offer to speak for them, for in doing so I am able to obtain a feel (incidentally, which I am unable to explain) before committing to a long-term financial marriage. The accuracy of this procedure can be attested to by the number of functional loans in the company's loan portfolio. There is not one single non-performing loan on the company's books.

The credit for the outstanding performance of these loans belongs to the kind heavenly Father. These loans are made a matter of prayer by the Provident staff. These prayers are coupled with a very thorough investigative process. The financial status and the repayment ability of each congregation are thoroughly examined and weighed in much the same way as banks and other lending institutions make their final determination. The collateral is usually not given as much weight and consideration as the manner in which the congregation is judged to be able to perform its financial obligations.

A trip to the Land of Caanan

After a series of meetings, examining plans, and being forcefully driven by the rapid increase caused by a growing congregation, the writer asked Pastor Manning to assemble a committee to travel to Panama City, Florida, for the purpose of visiting the last church he had built and pastored.

This church building was built by its founding pastor and 10 elderly brethren who were retired. The building was built within the time frame of 10 months with a seating capacity of 400 and with ample floor space to increase to a 500-plus capacity. This projection included the use of a balcony which would seat approximately 100 people.

When the pastor and committee arrived at 615 Tyndall

New Life

Parkway in Panama City, it was love at first sight! The building embraced most all the needs and wishes of the Valdosta congregation. A number of pictures and videos were taken of the "new Caanan" the spies had come to investigate. When they returned to Valdosta to share the good news with the anxious congregation, there was not one dissident in the crowd. I later told Pastor Manning that they had done a much better job than Joshua and Caleb, for the congregation believed the report! There were only two problems remaining, but with the faith and enthusiasm of the New Life Baptist congregation, these hurdles were to become stepping stones.

The services of a site planning engineer were sought, and he readily determined that the building would fit beautifully on the lot the church had purchased several months prior as a future building site. The widths and lengths on the building fulfilled critical dimensions which would allow for off-street parking on each side and to the rear of the building. A member of the building committee, Deacon Terry Kelly, expressed his satisfaction with the finished site plan as he viewed it for the first time. He flashed a giant size smile exposing one of the most perfect pearly white set of teeth in a shining ebony face and shouted loudly, "I love it when the Lord's plan comes together!" It obviously was the Lord's plan, for the entire plan met with unanimous approval from the church body. The only question asked was, "When can we get started?"

Another sixty-four thousand dollar question

There was a very popular game show which aired during the early days of television. The television host would direct a series of questions to a group of pre-selected participants. If they answered the questions correctly, they were given a sum of money. The main thrust of the show was climaxed when the finalist was asked the sixty-four thousand dollar question. The drums rolled, and the music accented the dramatic moment as the clearly stated question was given to the awestruck contestant. You could see everyone take a deep breath and wait to see if the correct answer could be given.

When I received the big $64,000 question from the New Life building committee, I could hear the drums rolling and the financial lights flashing as they asked, "Would Provident Investment Corporation lend the New Life congregation $600,000?" The requested amount was more than twice the amount we had loaned any congregation before. I was much like one of the fright-stricken contestants on the "Sixty Four Thousand Dollar Question" show. I turned up my spiritual hearing aid and asked them to restate the question! Surely enough, I heard them right...SIX HUNDRED THOUSAND DOLLARS! I don't need to tell you that when you invest that amount of money, you had better be sure that dog will hunt! We are talking about a monthly payment amounting to almost $6,000 for a 20-year period. Now you can see why I said a few sentences back that dog and hunter had better be ready to hunt.

To break that down in more simple terms, that's $1,500 that must come through those church offering plates each week, before paying the utility bills, pastor and staff salaries and the numerous other demands that are basic

Executive Committee: Shelvie Summerlin, President; Jon Ostrom, Vice President; Dr. G. Herfin Taylor, member; Frank Page, Secretary.

Shelvie Summerlin
signing loan check

Summerlin and Pastor Manning

Church Board, Summerlin, and Attorney Steve Guypton
at loan closing for New Life Baptist Church

177

to every congregation in America. I jestingly told Pastor Manning that he had better be sure he had heard from the throne room for he would be 65 years old when he made the last payment and that the payments would have to be made even if it took his social security check! We all had a good laugh, and I told them I personally did not have any problem with the loan, and I felt the executive committee would add their blessing by giving approval. The customary channels were followed, and each reviewing body concurred and was willing to lend its support to help build and finance a great soul-saving station in Valdosta, Georgia.

And away we go!

I have used this old cliche for many years, especially when embarking on a significant trip or work challenge. Even though this project was to be very consequential in the annals of Provident, I had been associated with projects over three times this size with a construction firm I owned a few years earlier. I felt very comfortable with our ability to supervise and oversee a project of this magnitude and even bigger if necessary. There was only one link in our chain that bore any chance of weakness, but when you stop to think that this is the Lord's church we are building, and He owns the cattle on a thousand hills, no one seemed to doubt that the church would pull the load! It was simply a matter of timing; and since none of us controlled the sunrise and sunset, we felt a unison urge and away we went!

Any project of major consequence must automatically expect hurdles and delays. Especially, if that effort is expected to be a viable force and pose a threat to Satan's kingdom. The church body Pastor Manning had put together under the leadership of the Holy Spirit possessed all the spiritual characteristics of upsetting the devil's apple cart!

I had seen the sizeable congregation crowd into the small church building on Mildred Street, and most of the time there were enough people to fill the building at least twice! The building had one small air conditioning unit that was capable of cooling the area for 50 people. Most of the time there were between 200 and 300 people present, and everyone had a red-hot testimony which automatically ignited when they came on the church grounds. New Life Baptist Church qualifies in more ways than one of being a red-hot church!

I mentioned hurdles and delays in a previous paragraph. I began my first church building project more than 40 years ago, and the first Imps I met from Satan's army were General Hurdle and Colonel Delay. These distinguished officers introduced themselves to me at that first building site, and since then they have been faithful visitors at every attempt I have made to build a church or to assist others. I have come to believe that hurdles and delays are an inseparable part of the building process, and anyone who joins the noble ranks of the Lord's advancing army should expect a generous amount of both. Patience is a virtue the building pastor must possess in generous supply.

The New Life congregation met every imaginable force of delay from the local building enforcement codes office to the grand-daddy of all hurdles and delays – the government's Environmental Protection Agency. Now if you are having difficulty figuring out what the EPA is, you don't need to waste your time, because the government does not have this dude defined yet. We were to learn in Valdosta that the federal government's agency would have to conduct an exhaustive study to determine what impact a growing church was going to have on the environment. We learned up front that EPA does not stand for Evangelical Preachers' Association. Nonetheless the bureaucracy was good for at least six months' worth of delays which kept the New Life congregation from advancing with their building project. However, on a positive note, souls continued to be saved until the congregation was forced to seek another building for worship purposes. Now hold your hat – the city fathers agreed to let them move to the Civic Center, where they continue at the time of this writing! The congregation had doubled in attendance in less than one year!

And it came to pass

I had assured Pastor Manning and the New Life congregation that I would not commit to any sizeable building project until such time as they resolved the obstacles to their church building project. Previous experience had taught me that this time element could be as much as one year or even more. We were virtually assured by the local building codes officials that the building permit would be issued as soon as the criteria was satisfied. With this assurance, tentative cost estimates were received from suppliers who were to provide the critical inner structure building components. Therefore, the delay period was used to some advantage to have these strategic supplies in place when the building began.

I usually do not share my private home telephone number with a lot of folks for obvious reasons. However, I had come to have close and comfortable experience with Pastor Larry Manning, and as a result of our growing Christian friendship, I had given him and Deacon Terry Kelly my home phone number and encouraged him to call. I guess I must have felt somewhat like the Apostle Paul felt, I was helping to groom a Timothy. I didn't want to miss the opportunity of being available if there was a chance of encouraging this promising young preacher. Both of us share similar lifestyles, and one of these is we are both early risers. Consequently, there is never a hesitancy from either of us to call in the early morning before daybreak. For years I have spent at least the first hour in the morning in meditation and Bible reading.

It was during one of these meditative encounters when the phone rang, and the excited voice of Pastor Manning shouted over Ma Bell's talking machine, "We got it! We got it!" After a few seconds when a reasonable amount of calm was restored, we both thanked the Lord for His faithfulness. A lesson that I have not learned too well even at my advanced age, is that the Lord's timing is not the same as man's. In reality the delays had been a real blessing. Our company had been able to complete a sizeable building project in Macon, Georgia, and other potential financial delays were resolved. Now we were ready to focus our total attention on a building that was needed very badly by a fast growing congregation in Lowdnes County.

Drive down the stakes, pull the building lines!

One of my "pet peeves" (whatever that means) has always been an "over attention effort" to foundational work. I learned a very valuable lesson in one of my first building attempts. If the foundation is not right, everything that happens during the building process must be adjusted to compensate for the margin of error. Therefore, I have always made it a near religious matter to be present when the engineering work for a foundation is being done. In fact, I carry a building transit level, complete with tripod and target, with me at all times when building sites and levels are to be determined and established. I jestingly refer to this type of work as subterranean excavating, engineering work. Sounds pretty fancy doesn't it? A few words about how this fancy term originated may be helpful.

More than 25 years ago when three of our five children were in college, I was extremely busy attempting to compete with heavy tuition costs and other incidental costs imposed by higher institutes of learning. One of my extra curriculars was to do foundation work on Fridays and Saturdays when two of my sons could help with this necessary work and also supply them with some much needed spending money. During one of these extended weekends, I had a sizeable single-story dwelling under contract and arranged to do the excavating work while I had two healthy boys to help me. The job was more than we could do in the allotted time frame so I rode over to the city unemployment office to seek some help.

Upon arriving, I saw several apparently able-bodied

African Americans waiting for a job opportunity, but I was to learn that they were discerningly adept at choosing the type of work they did, and ditch digging was not on their agenda. Four men came to my pickup and inquired about the type of work I had for them. When they learned that it was pick and shovel work in 100-degree temperatures, each one walked away and returned to the sidewalk pews while telling me, "No sir, we don't dig!" Somewhat angered by the lack of concern from these men who obviously needed work – and I was offering one dollar per hour above the minimum wage for foundation work – and unable to persuade one man to help me and my sons with what we thought was honorable work, I drove slowly away while observing the slothful disposition of able-bodied men who refused to work. I guess the reason I felt so bad was they had really outsmarted me.

On my way home one of Mr. Thomas Edison's miracles lit up in my mind as I remembered an old adage I had learned in personnel management school – "Work smarter, not harder!" As I pulled into the driveway, I observed my other pickup which remained loaded with several pieces of engineering equipment and a big plus, the truck was air conditioned. I parked under the shade tree along the side of the "engineering truck" and swapped vehicles and headed back toward the unemployment office.

When I arrived, the waiting men did not recognize me as the ditch-digging dude who just left, and several crowded up to the cab door as I pushed the down button to the electric-powered window. Unison inquiries came from the crowd, "Yes sir, boss, what kind of work do you want us to do?" To their question I replied, "Men, I need some help to do some subterranean excavating engineering work." They loaded up the truck. I was compelled to ask two men to get off because I had too many. As I drove off, I could see the assumed fortunate men smiling and working a "goody goody" finger at those poor souls who were left behind.

When we arrived at the job site, several miles from town, the men began to unload and select some of the engineering tools to work with. I told them to put the equipment back on the truck and I replaced the engineering wonder with a "one-man dragline," a shiny new true temper round point shovel. I told them we were going to do "subterranean excavating engineering work."

The distance of several miles back to the city that the men would have been required to walk, had they refused to work, was a plus I feel sure. But shortly all were engaged in pleasant chatter, and the sound of shovels and picks was heard as the foundation work progressed. About an hour after we had started to work, one of the more seasoned and personal laborers leaned on his shovel and yelled to me, "Hey Reb, what kinda work did you say we is doing?" I replied in a tone where I could conceal my inner laughter. "We are doing subterranean excavating engineering work." He mused for a moment and replied, "Well, I can tells you one thing, it is near bout like ditch digging." We all had a good laugh, and the joke was shared in a meaningful and productive manner. I hope I never have to go back to the unemployment office for some help to do my engineering work. I probably will be informed, "We don't dig!"

No problem – we dig

The ground-breaking day was a red letter day for the New Life congregation. This was a day when even the most humble church member could see that they were going to get a new church! The previous months of planning, financial meetings, and numerous other meetings meant little to them. Now they could see with their eyes, on land they owned, that something great and wonderful was about to happen!

When I arrived to assist with the foundation work, there were enough people present and ready to dig to build an army Quarter Master supply depot building. I have always built a very warm and personal relationship with every congregation I have worked with. New Life was no exception. Our relationship had advanced to the rock-solid stage insomuch that all of Pastor Manning's flock called me Pastor. I began the work day by telling the story I related in the previous paragraphs. I have never seen folks laugh so heartily. Deacon Terry Kelly walked over toward me with tears of joy in his eyes, giving me a hearty brotherly hug and said, "Yes sir, Pastor, we dig!"

Chapter Thirteen

Adjournment – Ad Interim

The time span I have spent in the drafting of this treatise has been in excess of two years. I never knew that a small literary effort could be so time consuming. My appreciation for other books I have read during this time has been greatly enhanced. Now I attempt to rise to the mammoth task of writing this closing chapter. This has been my greatest challenge thus far. How do you begin to close so great a story when new pages and chapters are unfurling daily? I am thoroughly convinced that the greatest story is yet to be told. Provident Investment Corporation is just moving into its most productive period, and the area of influence of this Christian-controlled financial institution is broadening constantly.

The history will be written by the organization regardless of whether or not the record is recorded on the printed page. That is why I have entitled this chapter Adjournment – Ad Interim which doubtless will be followed by greater stories, written in the path of progress as this company moves toward the close of the twentieth century. I fully believe that the greatest days of opportunity for the churches of Jesus Christ lie before us. The thunder of real revival can be heard in almost every nation of the earth as the body of Christ attempts to arise and meet the challenge of gathering the ripened harvest. These stories must be told and recorded in the safe pages of history to preserve them. Hopefully it will challenge those laborers who will work in the harvest fields until the Master returns and calls His church from all sections of the globe.

The challenge will increase

In the brief time that I have been working on the last two chapters of this book (less than a four-month period), a real revival has broken out in the New Life church. We have been forced to convert every possible square foot of floor space to a central worship area to house the fast-growing congregation. The total seating capacity at this time is approximately 600, and the church will not be able to house the congregation on its opening day of dedication! I have already suggested to Pastor Manning that he should begin to investigate the possibility of going to two services on Sunday mornings. This dual service system will at least buy some time for planning for an expansion system or possibly relocating the church to an area for greater amplitude.

The New Life story is just one of many that must be told, and for this reason and other greater stories, I strongly feel that there will be a sequel to this effort. I hope I shall be the one to share these thrilling and exciting testimonies through the medium of the printed page at a later date. While the many reports of buildings and church growth are exhilarating, there are other facets of this dramatic history that we have not been able to share because they have been dwarfed by miracles and wonders of growing and exciting churches.

From deficits to dividends

I possess a very thorough background in the field of accounting. I spent more than 25 years working for a large meat packing firm in this area, supervising a small network of offices manned by personnel who were charged with the responsibility of accounting for the various departments. It was during this time that I learned that accountability was one of the most important functions of any organization. It is the accounting reports which tell the real story about the health or ill being of the firm. The accounting process is not designed to make or lose money but rather to write the history in a series of figures. It is the job of management and leadership to interpret and assess these figures and chart the course for the organization they are leading.

The building and financing of churches is the meat and soul of Provident Investment Corporation. When both of these services are provided to churches, it is only reasonable to expect that the profits and bottom-line figures will reflect favorably for management and stockholders. Provident Investment Corporation has a body of stockholders which number more than 500. For a period of more than 15 years, they watched the price of their stock deteriorate to embarrassing levels before they were stabilized and began to climb upward in value. For the most part, they were understanding and mildly tolerant, but the management team who took the reigns of leadership in the last year of the '70s decade were dedicated from the onset to bring life and vitality to the firm they were to lead. In the decade of the '80s, the stock values rose more than 200 percent, and the miracle of miracles was about to take place.

Mr. Chairman, I move that we pay our stockholders a dividend

A group of shocked board of directors and a small assembled group of stockholders could hardly believe their ears as the slowly delivered words of the corporate secretary, Frank Page, rang out in the conference hall of the Holiday Inn in McDonough, Georgia, on July 20, 1993. "Mr. Chairman, I make a move that our corporation pay a dividend to our body of stockholders in the month of December this year." This was the first real red-letter day for any member of the body of stockholders. For the first time in almost 20 years, they realized that the corporation they had helped to fund for the purpose of financing churches for the kingdom of God was sound and well. Approximately $32,000 was going to be divided among approximately 500 members on the basis of share ownership. It was much like Neal Armstrong's first step on the moon – it was a giant step for mankind. This was indeed a giant step for a lending institution that had received new life as it had freed itself from the ashes of financial ruin.

Merry Christmas!

The board of directors decided that it would be especially rewarding to write the dividend checks and have the U.S. Postal Service deliver them the week before Christmas. This practice has been followed for a three-year period and is expected to continue and increase in the near future. I can speak from a personal standpoint that ole Santa's ride by the Summerlin house has been more pleasant and rewarding since Santa has been stuffing a much appreciated check in my Christmas stocking!

Obviously since there are approximately 500 people to share in the $30,000-plus dividend figure, none of the checks are very large. Conversely, the initial investments by the stockholders were not very large either even though some purchasers invested their lifetime savings. The sobering truth conveyed by mailing those first dividend checks was that the investments some very courageous folks had made a few years before were safe. The amount in the first check represented cash payment of approximately 5 percent of the book value of their stock. There was also another comforting truth which occurred but was not amply publicized – there was a comparable increase in the stock value! This increase in the stock value and a cash dividend payment represented about a 10 percent return on the stock's book value.

How big is big

Now if you are comparing the initial return of profits of Provident Investment Corporation stockholders to IBM, General Electric, General Motors, Ford or some of the other giants, you will doubtless be comparing a mole hill to a mountain. How big is big?

I looked up the meaning of the word big just to see what Mr. Webster had to say about the word. I found out that the meaning of the word was about as far reaching as a crisp frost on a cold December morning. Just consider some of Mr. Webster's suggestions of the word BIG. *Large in size, amount or scope, full to bursting; swelling, out-standingly worthy or able, important, imposing* and would you believe *pregnant!* Yes sir, that will catch your eyes and ears.

My dear old mother-in-law, who has been gone to the glory world for a number of years, was from the old school, and she avoided the use of many of Mr. Webster's words because they did not sound good in public. She was adverse to the word pregnant, so she used the old cliche "catched up," as a substitute to describe a lady when she was expecting a child. I do not intend to lose my reader while I am searching for a way to help avoid unfavorable comparison of this company's first effort with others who have been much more generous, so for lack of a better choice I'm going to borrow granny's cliche, we just got "catched up"; and while we are not as big as others, it was a giant step, and we really have just begun to walk! Incidentally, one of the meanings of "catched up" is "rich in significance."

I often find myself among those in the financial circles who revel in their accomplishments, and I have no problem with success when earned through the old "Smith-Barney" method. Recently, I was conversing with a loan officer who worked for a local bank that had met with laudable success. The young man strutted like a peacock because of his favorable association. If I remember correctly, a group of businessmen decided to form the bank, and those who were invited to participate had some very deep financial pockets. One member in particular, who was in the inner leadership circle, had a net worth in excess of $30 million. Many of the others were seven figure people and some with a modest high six figure base.

Now it does not take a Harvard lawyer to conjecture that if you have men with this kind of money, it is relatively easy to start a million dollar bank, and most folks would wager that the institution would grow and prosper if given sound leadership and guidance. The young man to whom I referred to earlier told me that in the space of less than 20 years they had grown to be a $38 million bank. I told him that the accomplishment was admirable; however, that instead of being a $38 million bank, they should be in excess of $100 million. He wanted to know why I thought they should have achieved such greatness. I replied that he had five men on the board who were personally worth more than the figure I had suggested!

You see, what I am attempting to say is, if you have almost unlimited resources, it is not too difficult to put together an institution of your dreams. However, if you have a dream and are unable to attract those with the clout I alluded to in the previous paragraph, you simply have to take your dream and begin with any who are willing to trust your fantasy. Be assured it will take more than a handful, especially if your dream goal is in the high seven figure column. If you are forced to go this way, your definition of the word *big* will be measurably different from those who work from a broader, more lucrative base. You might have to settle with just being "catched up" for being big!

The poor man's way takes a little longer

It is rare to find a person who does not have 20/20 hindsight vision or even better. I happen to be in that "even better" group. When I look back to the formative stages of this corporation, I think the greatest blunder that was made was the failure by the leadership body to recognize and respect the sacred trust that had been placed in them by poor people who had placed the only lamb they owned in their trust. I am unable to speak for our stockholder body at large, but I am intimately familiar with the members of our board of directors. Very candidly, we are not abundantly blessed with many seven figure personnel, and we must recognize that we simply have become a keeper of the sacred lamb.

David's abuse of the sacred lamb

There is a story in the II book of Samuel, Chapter 12 verses 1 through 23 which clearly outlines the attitude of God toward the sacred lamb. The story is available for all to read and to choose a proper personal posture for dealing with a sacred trust.

The story begins abruptly as the author introduces the preacher-prophet Nathan as being "sent by God" to King David to tell him a story about two men. One (representing King David) was very wealthy, owning many flocks and herds, and the other (representing Uriah the Hittite) a poor man, whom King David had slain and who owned one ewe lamb that he had bought and raised in his own house as a treasured pet. The writer of the sacred page declared, "The poor man had nothing, save one little ewe lamb."

The story continues by informing the reader that a (stranger) traveler came unto the rich man and was in need of food and shelter. The rich man was so selfish he refused to take one lamb from his abundant flocks to feed the hungry traveler, but rather TOOK the poor man's pet lamb and had it slaughtered to feed his guest. The story continues and is a great one, waiting for all to read, but due to space and time, let me sum it up by telling you that it got King David in a heap of trouble!

In no way do I intend to infer that it would be decorous to take anything from anyone regardless of their abundance or poverty, but if you are entrusted to take someone's sacred lamb, it had better be for a noble purpose and all the qualities of good and profound stewardship must come into play. You can always be sure that God has a prophet Nathan somewhere with omniscient understanding who knows every one of God's creation by name. This Guardian of truth knows the impecunious as well as the affluent, and He stands ready to thunder the wrath and judgment of a loving God upon those who abuse the sacred lamb! Let all mankind beware!

I noticed that I have got my hound dog running a rabbit that has taken us almost completely off course, but in the next few paragraphs, I will attempt to catch him and bring him back on course. There is a special trail that must be followed by those who are entrusted with the sacred lambs. The route is not as broad nor does it contain all the abundance of the moneyed. You can be assured that it takes a much greater effort to stay on the narrow path than the broad road of opulence.

Any money in the coffers?

"Just because there is money in the cash register, it does not necessarily mean that you are making money."

This deep and meaningful statement was lovingly and cautiously conveyed to me several years ago by a wise old banker-friend who made me a loan to begin a grocery story operation in a small south Georgia town. The prudent chief financial officer was mindful of the fact that the young man to whom he was making the loan was going to exchange a multitude of grocery items for cash. At the close of each day, there was going to be a large handful of money in the cash register. However, the only part that really belonged to me was the difference between the price I sold the items for, less the amount I had paid for them. Now sometimes when you take this last approach, it can leave some slim pickings in the cash drawer. All who have been in the grocery business will testify to the truth of the "slim pickings" method. But it is the only way for a grocer to survive; therefore, he must follow this principle unerringly if he is to survive. This axiom will apply to any business endeavor and may all who travel this path do so in wise trepidation.

Now all who know me very well know that I am a frugal soul. For this trait I doubtless owe a deep debt of gratitude to my parents. I was born in the late '20s and raised on a small rented farm during the great depression. I offer no apology for this because I learned if you got hold of a nickel, you had better hold on to it. I well remember the few times I got the treasured Indian-head nickel. I would visit every store in Moultrie, Georgia, with that nickel firmly gripped in my hand, deep in my right overall pocket. I would examine everything in each store that sold for five cents! Now you understand why I said earlier that I am a frugal soul. Again, no apology offered!

Another hindsight glance

Remember I told you earlier how good I am at hindsight surveillance? A close friend told me once that he was going to recommend me for the Nobel Peace Prize for outstanding performance in the field of "Hindsight Surveillance." Seriously, it did not require a college graduate with a degree in visionary perception to figure out that the dogs the founding leaders put out to hunt could not hunt, especially under the conditions employed at the time. The stock salesmen were all-out busy and each one bringing in a pocket full of money. The cash register was ringing loudly and frequently, but no one seemed to be able to make the essential determination: the only thing that really belonged to the company was the increase! An old accountant acquaintance of mine several years ago had a favorite saying, "There were too many ducks (deducts) in the pond." To name a few of the ducks that frequented the initiatory pond reservoir of Provident Investment Corporation were commissions, office overhead, salaries, travel expense, and a host of other ducks that gobbled up nearly all the revenues including the sacred lambs.

A necessary simple calculation

One of the main reasons I consented to the urging of the board of directors to attempt this literary effort was that I hoped to be able to present in a very simple readable style some of the integral elements which must be adhered to in the operation of any business. The heart and soul of America is the free enterprise system. Thousands of people each year challenge this vital entity, and many more go away threadbare, worn and disappointed than the number that succeeds. Some rise and flourish only to vanish in the pool of defeat simply because they were lured and enticed by the amount of money in the cash drawer. It makes no difference whether the money comes from a bank loan, personal savings, the sale of stock, or any other source, the person who will take the approach that it is a "sacred lamb" will not fail. He may be deprived of many conveniences and possibly bare necessities, but that person will emerge a victor.

A three-drawer cash register

In an earlier paragraph I adverted to an experience I had with a grocery store. Every effort was made from the onset to minimize investment cost. One of the cost control methods used was to buy all used equipment. The cash register was a must, and these babies could cost anywhere from a low of $50 to a high of $500 to $700 for one of the new National Cash Register model (NCR). The top of the line had the capacity not only to tabulate a grocery market list but to code cost. At the end of each working day, the machine would give you the total intake plus the cost of goods sold. I convinced myself that the $50 route was the way to go, so I bought an old National Cash Register that had a top ring out of $3. If you sold a customer a supply of grocery and market items for $11, you simply rang the $3 lever three times and the $2 lever once. I surely did enjoy hearing the clerks ring that old cash register lever. Occasionally someone would buy a $20 order, and the store would sound much like the gambling casino I saw on television when someone hit the jackpot. Never mind the comparison, but it was sweet music to my ears.

As much as I enjoyed the ring of the old cash register, there were some other characteristics that could have been damaging if I had not been trained in thriftiness by the Herbert Hoover administration during the early 30's. I don't aim to blame the National Cash Register for my brief life (three years) in the grocery business, but the things that were wrong with the cash register I had were: 1) There was only one drawer. 2) The machine was capable of giving one total each day, and that was the total intake. In hindsight from the current vantage point, what I really needed was a register with three drawers and a machine that was capable of tabulating the total income and computing the cost of the goods that were sold. Had I purchased the more expensive machine, I would have known at the close of each business day exactly where I stood. Then I could have divided the money into two parts. One for the suppliers I owed for the store supplies and the remainder belonged to me as profit for my services. The top drawer would be emptied at the end of the day. The third drawer (much or little) was mine.

As homespun as the account I have just given may appear, it is still a sound foundation upon which to operate any business. Today Provident is a million dollar-plus corporation with a sound financial base upon which can be built for many years to come. We have the leadership and staff who have the dedication and resolve to lead this organization into the future and doubtless will be the largest church lending institution in America. There are four things I want us to continue to do (1) Under no circumstances spend out the top cash register drawer; (2) Guard the second drawer like a sacred lamb for it does not belong to us; (3) Exercise sound stewardship over the third drawer, for this represents the sacred trust the stockholder body has earned through its trusted leadership and staff; (4) Give all praise and honor for all accomplishments to God the Father, God the Son, and God the Holy Spirit. For without Him we could not have endured the valleys and would not have known how to climb the mountain. I don't know about you, but I came up on the right side of the mountain. Most of the members of the board of directors have the battle scars to prove it. There is one lesson we have learned well: keep your eyes on all three of the cash register drawers, invest wisely, and guard the company assets as if they were our own!

Staff: Ralph Summerlin, Henry Wright II, Shelvie Summerlin, Betty Reese, Jon Ostrom, Debbie Sanders, Dr. G. Herfin Taylor, Bobby Tatum, and Frank Page.

Pastor Henry Wright II greeting the stockholders.

Stockholders' meeting – August 20, 1996.